TEACHING SECONDARY SCHOOL LITERACIES WITH ICT

Learning and Teaching with Information and Communications Technology

Series Editors: Anthony Adams and Sue Brindley

The role of ICT in the curriculum is much more than simply a passing trend. It provides a real opportunity for teachers of all phases and subjects to rethink fundamental pedagogical issues alongside the approaches to learning that pupils need to apply in classrooms. In this way it foregrounds the ways in which teachers can match in school the opportunities for learning provided in home and community. The series is firmly rooted in practice and also explores the theoretical underpinning of the ways in which curriculum content and skills can be developed by the effective integration of ICT in schooling. It addresses the educational needs of the early years, the primary phase and secondary subject areas. The books are appropriate for pre-service teacher training and continuing professional development as well as for those pursuing higher degrees in education.

Published and forthcoming titles:

Adams & Brindley (eds): *Teaching Secondary English with ICT*
Barton (ed.): *Teaching Secondary Science with ICT*
Florian & Hegarty (eds): *ICT and Special Educational Needs*
Johnston-Wilder & Pimm (eds): *Teaching Secondary Maths with ICT*
Loveless & Dore (eds): *ICT in the Primary School*
Monteith (ed.): *Teaching Primary Literacy with ICT*
Monteith (ed.): *Teaching Secondary School Literacies with ICT*
Way & Beardon (eds): *ICT and Primary Mathematics*

TEACHING SECONDARY SCHOOL LITERACIES WITH ICT

Edited by
Moira Monteith

Open University Press

Open University Press
McGraw-Hill Education
McGraw-Hill House
Shoppenhangers Road
Maidenhead
Berkshire
England
SL6 2QL

email: enquiries@openup.co.uk
world wide web: www.openup.co.uk

and Two Penn Plaza, New York, NY 10121-2289, USA

First Published 2005

A catalogue record of this book is available from the British Library

ISBN 0 335 21346 4 (pb)   0 335 21347 2 (hb)

Library of Congress Cataloging-in-Publication Data
CIP data applied for

Typeset by RefineCatch Limited, Bungay, Suffolk
Printed in the UK by MPG Books Ltd, Bodmin, Cornwall

CONTENTS

CONTRIBUTORS

Geoff Barton began teaching English at Garforth Comprehensive School, Leeds, in September 1985. He is currently Headteacher at King Edward VI School in Suffolk. In 1986 he was asked to write a textbook about language skills and since then he has written around 40 English text books. He also writes and lectures on literacy, behaviour management and school leadership.

Sue Brindley is currently a Lecturer in Education at the University of Cambridge, where she is course manager for the secondary PGCE and leads the English PGCE. She also coordinates the MEd module on Researching Practice: Early Career Teachers. She is general editor of the forthcoming Open University Press series on teaching and ICT and co-author of the volume on secondary English teaching with ICT. Before this post, she was Professional Officer for English at QCA, and wrote the Open University Secondary English PGCE.

Charles Crook is Reader in Education at the University of Nottingham, where he is attached to the Learning Sciences Research Institute. His research takes a cultural psychological perspective on young people's use of new technology.

Roy Dymott was a graduate student at Loughborough University and now works in industry.

Kwok-Wing Lai is an Associate Professor and Head of the Faculty of Education, University of Otago. He has a keen interest in studying and researching into the use of computer-mediated communication in the school curriculum, teacher development, as well as the social and ethical aspects of ICT use in education. He is the founding editor of *Computers in New Zealand Schools*.

Guy Merchant, after teaching for many years, now coordinates the work of the Language and Literacy Research Group in the School of Education at Sheffield Hallam University. He has published widely in the area of curriculum English and is particularly interested in the impact of new technology on the ways in which we define and use literacy. He is currently researching the use of onscreen writing in the early years.

Moira Monteith is currently an educational consultant and was previously principal lecturer in ICT in education at Sheffield Hallam University and before that an English teacher. She has written and edited a number of books concerned with the use of ICT and with writing. Recent research includes student use of a 'virtual campus' at Sheffield Hallam University and student web-based study.

Sarah Monteith received a BA hons in English Literature from Lancaster University, and a PGCE in middle years education from Edge Hill University College. She is currently teaching English to years 7 to 11 at Lathom High School, a mixed comprehensive in Skelmersdale, Lancashire. She has taught the literacy summer school at Lathom and is the ICT coordinator for the English Department there.

Rachel Pilkington (C.Psychol., ILTM) is a Senior Lecturer in ICT and manages the e-learning team at the School of Education, University of Birmingham. Rachel received a B.Sc. in Psychology from York University in 1984 and a Ph.D. in Education from the Computer Based Learning Unit, University of Leeds, in 1988. She has researched dialogue in a variety of computer-based and networked learning contexts from developing literacy in disadvantaged school children to tutoring diagnostic skills in medicine and developing communities of practice in education.

Chris Turner lectures at Manchester Metropolitan University's Institute of Education, mainly as a member of the Secondary English Team. Before joining the university, he was a Head of English in a Stockport compre-hensive school. He has research interests in and has written about ICT and English, and literacy theory and reading.

Alison Tyldesley lectures at the Institute of Education, Manchester Metropolitan University. Previously she was a Literacy Consultant for Derbyshire LEA and before that a classroom teacher.

Aisha Walker has a degree in Linguistics from the University of Lancaster, an MEd in Educational Technology/TESOL from the University of

Manchester and a Ph.D. in Education from the University of Leeds. She is now based at the University of Leeds, where she teaches ICT in Education and conducts research into e-learning and computer-mediated discussion. Aisha is also a qualified teacher with several years of classroom experience working with different age groups.

Noel Williams is Head of Art, Design, Communications and Media at Sheffield Hallam University, as well as Reader in Communications, with major research interests in the overlaps between ICT and human communication. He was one of the founders of the UK Writing and Computers Society, and established Hallam's MAs in Technical Communication, Professional Communication and e-Communication. Currently his main research preoccupations are the evaluation of Voice Recognition systems, computer games as discourse, and the discourse cross-overs between different new media, especially in popular culture and the teaching of communication skills.

SERIES EDITORS' INTRODUCTION

The publication in the UK in 1975 of the Bullock Report (HMSO), deliberately ambiguously named *A Language for Life*, marked a turning point in thinking about the teaching of English. It was the first full-scale study of the field since the earlier, and equally influential, Newbolt Report, *The Teaching of English in England* (HMSO, 1926).

As their titles and terms of reference suggest, both reports were primarily concerned with the teaching of what we now have come to call 'Subject English', itself a recognition that the demands for thinking about 'English' or 'language' go far beyond the concerns that have been traditionally seen as the concern of the English teacher, especially at secondary and tertiary level. Some recent research (1998) (Bethan Marshall and Sue Brindley, *Changing English*, 5.2) suggests that primary and secondary schoolteachers construe their understanding of what is timetabled as 'English' in very different ways; a point to which we return later. In the Guidance document, *Framework for Teaching English: Years 7, 8 and 9* (that is ages 11–13), published by the Department for Education and Employment (2001), this confusion seems replicated with an uncertainty whether it is speaking of a whole school language policy or 'Subject English'.

But both Newbolt and Bullock show themselves well aware of the issues implicit here. A prominent member of the Newbolt committee was George Sampson who, in his influential book, *English for the English* (Cambridge University Press, 1921), wrote the memorable phrase: 'Every

teacher *in* English is a teacher *of* English' (our emphasis). Similarly there was a brief but influential chapter in Bullock (Chapter 12, pp. 188–93) entitled, *Language Across the Curriculum.*
The introductory paragraph to this chapter (12.1) reads as follows:

> In the . . . preceding chapters we have made several references to the role of language in other areas of the curriculum than English. It became clear to us in the early days of the inquiry that we could not do justice to the . . . term[s] of reference if we did not address our remarks to *all* teachers, whatever their subject [original emphasis]. Indeed, we believe that the suggestions made . . . for improving the teaching of language could result in more effective teaching of subjects that lie right outside the terms of reference [that is the teaching of English].

The rest of Chapter 12 expands on this theme and essentially echoes the sentiments of George Sampson.
Brief though it was, Chapter 12 of Bullock led to a huge range of publications on the theme of 'language across the curriculum', or 'LAC' as it came to be known in virtually every English-speaking country. With hindsight, it might be argued that it was by far the most influential and enduring aspect of the Report's findings.
Two principles seemed to emerge in many of these documents. First, language development and awareness was a responsibility for every teacher in the school, not one to be restricted to the English department. Second, for this to be effective, schools should appoint a language coordinator, responsible for in-service education in the language area, and, frequently, the Head of English was not necessarily the best placed person to undertake this role.
LAC, as a concept, would hardly be recognized these days but, in many ways, our current concerns with 'literacy', with which this book deals, derive from the awareness of the need for whole school language policies and planning which Bullock stressed.
The other key finding from the research and development work in the LAC area in the 70s and 80s of the last century was that it was a concept which found a more fruitful uptake in primary schools than, generally, in secondary schools. This largely resulted from the class teacher based pattern of primary education as opposed to the subject-based pattern of most secondary schools, something which, in England and Wales, has been exacerbated by the introduction of the National Curriculum with its emphasis on subject knowledge. The primary teacher is more enabled to keep an eye on the student's language development as a whole and can intervene helpfully where problems arise in whatever curriculum area.
There is indeed some evidence from test results that many students regress in literacy terms after the transition from primary to secondary schools. It is partly for this reason, apart from her own skills as an editor,

that we invited Moira Monteith to edit this volume in the series, as a complement to her earlier book, *Teaching Primary Literacy with ICT*. There is no other area in the curriculum where continuity across phases is more important and we hope that the two books can be read together with each informing the reading of the other.

We welcome, therefore, the extension of the now well-established 'literacy hour' in English primary schools, where the reports of the Office for Standards in Education (Ofsted) show it to have been largely successful in improving literacy standards, to the secondary phase also. But it becomes ever more important to interpret the concept of literacy far beyond the simplistic concept of 'barking at print', what Seymour Papert has characterized in *The Children's Machine* as 'letteracy'.

We would also argue that, as with the earlier LAC movement, 'literacy' must not be seen as a major responsibility for the English department alone.

In the technically rich world of the twenty-first century the demands of literacy have changed and widened as we have argued in the introduction to Moira's previous volume in the series. The point has been well made in a significant paragraph in the successor to Bullock, The Kingman Report on the Inquiry into the teaching of English Language (HMSO, 1988):

> Round the city of Caxton, the electronic suburbs are rising. To the language of books is added the language of television and radio, the elliptical demotic of the telephone, the processed codes of the computer. As the shapes of literacy multiply, so our dependence on language increases. But if language motivates change, it is itself changed. To understand the principles on which that change takes place should be denied to no one.
>
> *(op.cit. 2.7)*

Our only gloss on this would be that much has happened since 1988 and, arguably, many people have moved in the meantime from 'the city of Caxton' to 'the electronic suburbs' which makes the role of ICT in relation to literacy studies ever more important in and across the curriculum context.

Interestingly enough, in a later chapter, Kingman returns in a major recommendation to the now well-worn aspect of LAC:

> The Committee recommends that all primary schools should have a member of staff who is designated as a language consultant, and who has the responsibility for advising on and co-ordinating language work, including knowledge about language.
>
> (4.52)

and

The Committee recommends that all subject departments concerned with the teaching of language in secondary schools . . . develop a co-ordinated policy for language teaching.

(4.51)

It is to these issues that the present volume addresses itself. Moira and her contributors look at the entitlement of students to a wider extension of the understanding of literacy in the twenty-first century. They also look at the way in which ICT can be used to extend the teaching of traditional literacy skills.

But there is also one important additional element. Of the nine chapters presented here, no fewer than four are concerned in a secondary context with literacy beyond the classroom and outside the formal boundaries of schooling. As students, and indeed their teachers, widen their experience of, and come to rely more on, electronic communications (emails and bulletin boards), chatrooms and the internet, new possibilities open up. As much learning now goes on outside, or beyond, the conventional classroom as within.

In assembling the range of contributors who comprise this volume, Moira Monteith has succeeded in setting an agenda for literacy in the secondary school for the twenty-first century.

Anthony Adams & Sue Brindley

INTRODUCTION

Moira Monteith

This book deals with the challenges in our society's drive towards full literacy and with changes in language use, alongside its overall brief to be concerned with Information Communications Technology (ICT) and literacy. It focuses on secondary school learning and the great potential in young people's use of ICT at home. All contributors consider the relationship between technology and literacy within specific contexts, and, as Charles Crook and Roy Dymott suggest in Chapter 6, with the interaction of systems of behaviour rather than the separate categories of ICT and literacy.

Use of ICT nowadays is wide-ranging, so in this introduction I take two examples that indicate the spread of impact. The first one concerns the more immediately obvious connections between text-messaging and teenagers' writing; the second may reveal rather more subtle indications of change, the impact of ICT on the design of dictionaries. The first has obvious and immediate connections which show up within the classroom; the second is happening now and may well have results we cannot at this moment entirely foresee. The introduction then considers the position of literacy within the secondary curriculum in general. Finally, the chapters are briefly outlined so that readers can appreciate the overall direction of the book.

The right to literacy (and ICT?)

Mass use of ICT can be considered now as part of the general context of language use in the developed world. In the two most populous countries where English is taught as a main language course, the United States and United Kingdom, computers and allied technology are common in work-place, schools and homes. Both the US and UK are attempting to make progress in their education policies to grant everyone, that is, as nearly as possible 100 per cent of the population, access to literacy. Not that this is a new effort:

> [In 1970] the Right to Read Effort was established with the purpose of ensuring that by 1980 99 per cent of all Americans under 16 and 90 per cent of all over 16 would have functional literacy.
>
> (DES 1975)

We are used to hearing about 'mass media', 'mass audiences' and even 'mass literacy'. But 'mass' does not mean 'total' and it appears to be the functional literacy of society as a whole that is so difficult to achieve. *A Language for Life* was the first major report in England and Wales focusing on children's language development both in schools and also within the wider society. In fact, the *Language for Life* report was originally commissioned to find out whether or not pupils' reading scores in state schools were going down. The brief was widened to include aspects of language development and the report found that there was no need for panic as regards the more able pupils, though there was a long tail of pupils with poor attainment in writing and reading.

When the National Foundation of Educational Research undertook reviews of evidence prior to the establishment of the National Literacy Strategy they found: 'standards in literacy among British primary school children have largely remained stable over the period between 1948 and 1996' (DfEE 1999). Of course, that was good news from the point of view of maintaining standards, but it does seem to imply that some different input is required to move from 'mass literacy' to a situation of almost 100 per cent literacy. Indeed, the evidence arising from recent literacy initiatives has been slightly disappointing also in terms of the elusory goal of 99 per cent success.

Naturally, we all look for solutions to improve matters. One of the questions this book tries to answer is whether or not ICT will make a quantitative, or indeed a qualitative, difference in terms of mass literacy.

The impact (assault?) of technology

Some people feel that ICT brings its own problems with it. 'Some teachers see the creeping abbreviations as part of a continuing assault of technology on formal written English' (Lee 2002). Jennifer Lee's article about teaching English in the United States highlighted features of an apparently continuous process: the ever closer connections between oral and written forms of language. They have always been connected, of course, and education reports such as *A Language for Life* (DES 1975: 63) made this abundantly clear. 'Into this context of purposeful, sociable and consolidating talk, the infant teacher introduces the written language. What it brings is fresh material to be talked about, for the spoken word must mediate the written.' New technologies as such did not at that time figure very much in the relationship, although the report did discuss the effect of television, finding the case not proven in terms of whether or not its effects were adverse as regards literacy learning (DES 1975: 13).

When ownership of computers became more widespread, a general argument arose in the UK as to whether or not English teachers and Examination Boards should permit the use of word processors by pupils (see Chapter 3), but the focus remained on written language as we then understood it. Now the situation has changed. Computers are much more sophisticated and the connections between computers, phones and cameras much closer. Forms of language can be interchanged more easily than ever before. We can type text into a word processor and listen to it read back aloud; we can have our speech recorded then changed into written format that can be read on a screen or printed on paper.

Two apposite articles, drawn originally from the *New York Times*, appeared in the business pages of the *International Herald Tribune*, 21 September 2002. A journalist, Jennifer Lee, interviewed American teachers and students just beginning the new term in school. In Illinois an English teacher, Jaqueline Harding, prepared for the following year's work by drawing up a list of 'the common writing mistakes' she saw in her students' written work, a familiar procedure used by many English teachers. After all, it seems highly appropriate to use the students' own writing to explain to them what is considered acceptable and what is not. Ms Harding's 'traditional' list of student mistakes will be recognized immediately by all teachers: *There, their, they're. Your, you're. To, too, two. Its, it's.* However, this year she added to the list items from a new form of practice she had noticed being used frequently by her students: *u, r, ur, b4, wuz, cuz, 2.* Several teenagers who were interviewed for the newspaper article said that:

they use instant-messaging shorthand without thinking about it. They write to one another as much as they write in school, or more. . . . Almost 60 per cent of the online population under age 17 uses instant

messaging, according to Nielsen/NetRatings. . . . abbreviations are a
natural outgrowth of this rapid-fire style of communication. . . . For
[teenagers] expressions like 'o i c' (oh I see), 'nm' (not much), 'jk' (just
kidding) and 'lol' (laughing out loud), 'brb' (be right back), 'ttyl' (talk to
you later) are as standard as conventional English.

(Lee 2002)

No doubt, many of the 'trendy' words used by generations of adolescents
are either now accepted in mainstream English or are totally forgotten,
most likely the latter. If such words occurred in essays or written work
for school, the words most probably were underlined by the teacher as
indicating disapproval. Students would have understood, even if they
argued the case, that such words belonged to conversations with peers
but not in school work. 'Teenage' language used to be a form of spoken
English. Now it includes a great deal of writing – as the journalist noted,
as much if not more than the total they write for school.

The second feature in the same issue of the *Herald Tribune* concerned
emoticons (including smiley and not smiley faces).

Scott Fahlman, a computer scientist at Carnegie Mellon University
posted an email on a university bulletin board system suggesting that a
colon, a minus sign and a parenthesis be used to convey a joking tone.
   The message was brief:
   'I propose the following character sequence for joke markers: : -)
   Read it sideways. Actually it is probably more economical to mark
things that are NOT jokes, given current trends. For this, use : – ('

(Hafner 2002)

Now, after 20 years, the spreading use of such hieroglyphs appears to
have had a remarkable impact on teenagers.

Even terms that cannot be expressed verbally are making their way into
papers. Melanie Weaver, a teacher in Pennsylvania stated: 'they would
be trying to make a point in a [school assignment] paper, they would put
a smiley face in the end. If they were presenting an argument and they
needed to present an opposite view, they would put on a frown.'

(Lee 2002)

These features of teenage 'writing' may not matter. Perhaps we can still
school our students away from using smiley faces and even to remember
to write 'because' instead of 'cuz' or 'cos'. But the interlinking of oral/
written language continues and must impact on future expressions of
literacy and our working definitions of literacy. Perhaps our view of

literacy itself may change, or we might include a sub-variant connected with 'texting' rather as we include a range of dialects within spoken language. We need to discuss these implications with our students now in school.

Dictionaries and computers

ICT has had an impact already on how we monitor language change. It used to be considered the rule that dictionaries tended to slow down the rate of change as users would look up word meanings and stick with those. The evolution of meaning would then slow down similarly. If you wanted to find out the etymology or history of a word, you could look it up in a large, comprehensive dictionary and all the uses of particular words would be listed there with references as they had been found in books or writing of some description. The first use of a word notated within this system might not be the one you were looking for at all.

Merely a few years ago people had the onerous task of typing in entire texts and checking them as they did so. Complete novels by authors such as Dickens and Austen were keyed into various computer programs. It was only when scanning devices had effective translating software that typing whole books became a redundant chore. Once texts had been keyed in, however, the search possibilities available had widened tremendously. Similarly, the development of databases had important results in terms of capacity, making information easily available in an online dictionary or one on CD-ROM. (Word processors accompanied by a thesaurus still tend to be rather weak in comparison, though still useful.) As new collections of print, including newspapers and other fairly ephemeral publications, came online the collection of material became even easier. It was obvious that meanings or senses of words were different in different English-speaking countries and also that contemporary usage might be different from that of previous centuries, so in this sense ICT has helped dictionaries keep up with current usage. As a result, current language usage and varieties of English are now given more importance than in previous centuries and therefore senses of words can be updated more easily.

It seems useful at this point to ask for expert opinion, so I include here an email from Edmund Wright, Database Manager at Bloomsbury Publishing plc and main programmer of the Encarta World English Dictionary (EWED).

1) Order of definitions.
The old rule, pioneered by the Oxford English Dictionary (OED), was to order definitions by date of first usage, with the earliest first; and other dictionaries (including, of course, Oxford's other products, which dominated the market until the 1970s) followed where the OED led. More recent dictionaries have

adopted the rule of generally ordering senses by frequency of usage, with the most common first; indeed, it would now be very perverse for a new dictionary to use any other system. The Collins English Dictionary (CED), first published in 1979, was the first major British dictionary to use this rule, which was one of its major selling points. The logic is that this order is more likely to be convenient for the reader. Ordering by date of first usage is very useful if you're doing language research, but not if you want to look up the meaning of a word. The odds are that the sense you want is one of the ones still in general use, which in many cases are not the oldest ones; therefore, you would often have to read through several obsolete senses before you reached the right one. Ordering by frequency means you will find the sense you want faster, because it will probably be near the beginning of the entry.

2) Uses of computers, databases, etc., in making definitions
Modern dictionary production wouldn't be possible without the growth of IT. The most high-profile case is the use of corpora: large collections of books, newspapers, transcripts of spoken English, etc., held on computer in such a way that they can quickly be retrieved and analyzed. The construction and use of corpora is a huge subject; but, put very simply, their purpose from a lexicographer's point of view is that the division of a word or phrase into its different senses and the definition of those senses – and, indeed, the relative frequency of those senses – can now be tested against a much larger quantity of evidence than was possible previously. Nor do corpora any longer have to be kept on large expensive systems: modern PCs can easily hold a corpus of many millions of words.

However, there have been other equally important benefits. In general, as in so many other areas, the phenomenal growth in cheap computing power enables us to do things faster and better, thus speeding up the editorial cycle and production of the book, and allowing us to be more ambitious in what we attempt. The CED, using the IT technology of the time, took about six years of work to complete; the Encarta World English Dictionary (EWED; first published by Bloomsbury and Microsoft in 1999), took two and a half years to create a single unified database from which was produced both a British English and an American English version, each both in print and on CD.

Two specific examples:
1) The principle of a 'unified database' is that each sense exists only once in the database, with US/UK differences being noted by special coding – very much cheaper than writing two complete books in parallel. Another benefit is a virtual guarantee that the two versions are consistent, because they use as much of the same data as possible. The necessary coding is simple in theory, if intricate in practice. When it's all properly set up, an output program can automatically produce a US or a UK dictionary. This approach would be impossible in a non-computerized setting.

Incidentally, one type of US/UK variation ties in directly with the sense-order question. The relative frequency of senses often differs between American and British English; therefore, the same database records needed to manifest in a different order in the American and British versions of EWED.

2) EWED was compiled by a world-wide team of freelance lexicographers and advisors, working at home on sections of the database. They were located mainly in the UK and the USA, but also in South Africa, Australia, etc. This would have been impossible without: (a) the Internet and email, for easy communication and exchange of data; (b) the spread of cheap computing power, so we could rely on all contributors having a PC to run the software we provided to edit the data. This meant that each definition could be edited by both British and American lexicographers, looking at it from the point of view of their own variety of English; and the result was that each version of EWED was genuinely written by native speakers of that variety. By contrast, previous dictionaries have been compiled by a comparatively small team of lexicographers working in one place. Assembling such a multinational team would have been prohibitively expensive, and so previous dictionaries have been very much either British or American.

Clearly the effects of ICT on dictionary compilation will continue and will expedite the collection of varieties of English that will go to make up the 'global' language it is fast becoming. It does mean also that the use of those words that are generally acceptable in formal contexts, or what is termed 'Standard English', will not be uniform throughout English-speaking countries.

Current literacy practice

Literacy itself changes our world view. When we are literate, we no longer have to depend only on the people we know and meet for knowledge but can move beyond our immediate circle. Most people consider literacy to be a necessary, inevitable and generally enlightening threshold through which we must pass. But in England a surprisingly large minority apparently do not accept literacy as an essential way of knowing while at school and manage to get by with various levels of subliteracy. Yet our country is managed on the basis of full literacy. For example, people are expected to understand various forms such as tax and benefit forms, some of which require quite high reading ability yet must be tackled in order to obtain awards and allowances.

We have a relatively poor showing with regard to literacy compared with many other European countries (DfEE 1999: 9) and some critics complain about this on the grounds of the lower employability of barely literate people (DfEE 1999: 25). It is certainly true that a large number of inmates in jail have very low literacy scores at intake, but presumably that is not the only reason the individual ends up in jail but one of a series of difficulties he or she has had to work through.

Teachers have realized for many years that some pupils coming into secondary schools were not literate, and individual schools and local education authorities have instituted specialist teaching with regard to literacy. However, there was no overall policy on this matter before the National Literacy Strategy. This lack of coordination may have resulted partly from the general notion many of us had that pupils should become literate in their primary school phase. Not all do so, and thus the problem of subliteracy has perpetuated itself. At the moment we have a number of ongoing national initiatives and strategies concerned with literacy from the ages of 5 to 14. These post-primary phase initiatives involve pupils who do not have very deeply embedded literacy skills on entering secondary school and also adults who have gone through all their years in education and still remain largely lacking in basic skills. Even so, we are not entirely efficient in this respect nor single-minded in our planning.

I quote from two people involved in teaching literacy post-11, who were speaking not to other English teachers but to a more general audience. They indicate that we are certainly prioritizing literacy but not financing it sufficiently and that the emphasis on literacy is only one new priority among many. Sue Colquhoun, a lecturer at Croydon College, stated: 'There are seven million adults in the UK with the literacy and numeracy skills of 11-year-olds, and the government has set FE college targets to raise standards. The government is putting money into initiatives, but the cash is not going to the lecturers' (Colquhoun 2002). Similarly, in prison education targets are set for education providers within the terms of their contracts. This has the effect that staff perhaps focus only briefly on literacy in this or that institution as the contracts are for a short period of time (Braggins 2001: 17).

Very recent research appears to reinforce a move back towards motivating pupils and adults towards enjoyment in reading, in order to encourage the development not only of basic skills but more long-term achievement. The Literacy Trust website states that:

> New analysis of research by the Programme for International Student Assessment (PISA) on the reading skills of 15-year-olds has found that, 'being more enthusiastic about reading and a frequent reader was more of an advantage than having well educated parents in good jobs.'
> PISA measures how well young adults nearing the end of compulsory schooling are prepared to meet the challenges of modern life. The researchers conclude that working to engage students in reading may be one of the most effective ways to break cycles of educational and social disadvantage.
>
> (Literacy Trust 2002a)

Also, there has been an evaluation of the initiative involving both libraries and adult basic skills training:

> The evaluation of the Vital Link libraries and adult basic skills initiative, run in partnership by the Literacy Trust, the National Reading Campaign and The Reading Agency, . . . carried out by researchers at the University of Sheffield, recommended that the adult basic skills core curriculum be amended to include a focus on reading for pleasure and reader development, 'offering support and choice to facilitate self-direction'.
>
> (Literacy Trust 2002b)

The findings concur with the recommendations in *Shared Responsibilities* (Braggins 2001: 24) on widening the education currently available to most prisoners.

However, there remains the matter of priorities. Leigh Hughes, head of the English department at a comprehensive school wrote to the *Guardian* newspaper 15 August 2002, describing how he saw the current context of language learning within secondary schools.

> It is mid-August, so we have the traditional questioning of the reliability of A-levels. . . . I will return in September to begin a year which will involve teaching and managing the second year of the new national literacy strategy for years seven to nine, a year-nine curriculum which will lead to a new keystage three exam, in May, and a new year 10 to 11 GCSE curriculum to be examined for the first time in 2004. Parents, teachers and, most importantly, pupils do not need further change creating uncertainty and undermining confidence. We need a period of five years in which there are no new 'strategies' or 'initiatives', in which teachers and pupils can concentrate on learning, rather than coping with ever-changing regulations, specifications and small print.

Concurring with this attitude, most teachers, lecturers and those staff concerned with prison education ask emphatically for a hiatus in the rate of curricular change (Braggins 2001: 24).

One of the nubs of the matter must certainly be: *coping with ever-changing regulations, specifications and small print*. It is true that those concerned with planning National Curricula need to look at the principles behind change, and the over-riding long-term needs of the students. But even if government strategists were to agree to a temporary cessation in the introduction of new educational initiatives or targets, we know that ICT keeps changing and so will youngsters' use of it. As teachers, surely, we need to focus more effectively on the relationship of ICT and literacy and the changes that will bring rather than on 'ever-changing regulations'. If we think for a moment about what happened with the introduction of print we know that the changes brought about with the use of ICT will be both considerable and long-term. The challenge is threefold:

- we need to decide what is important among all the initiatives with regard to literacy;
- ensure that staff are there to help and encourage student learning;
- decide how to use ICT as the new literacy technology.

This book gives us a baseline, helping us ascertain where we are now (although some of you will find it is inevitably already out of date) and suggests ways for future development. The chapters are organized so that the guiding ideas move from the transition stages Key Stages 2 to 3, the policies behind literacy in the secondary curriculum, discussion as to what this curriculum should be in the light of current developments in ICT, projects currently in use, including one using computer mediated communication (CMC) in the classroom. Chapter 6 convincingly views both language and ICT as systems of activities and suggests that literacy activities will become more socialized in future. The next two chapters focus on the literacy implications involved in computer games, with a group of young male teenagers and also chatrooms with young females. In both cases, the social nature of the literacy acitivities is evident. Finally, the book concludes with what parents and children are doing about using the internet and the implicit literacy skills involved; it stresses the need for the development of evaluation skills.

Moira and Sarah Monteith in the first chapter see ICT as the latest literacy technology and that in itself means we need to use it as part of our literacy work. It is not just a matter of learning to use ICT to promote literacy or explore literacy sources. ICT can be pencil and paper, paint and canvas, chisel and stone. It provides possibilities for collaborative work: projects using 'exploratory talk' and involving ICT have promoted 'a way of using language for thinking together which is valued highly in most societies'. As a very practical aid, ICT could bring more continuity across the institutional break which children in the UK experience at the age of 11 and which appears to have at least a temporary effect on their standards of achievement. ICT can encourage collaboration between primary and secondary schools both in exchange of work and the development of 'new cognitive demands' in year 6, as recommended in the QCA report (2002). The writers believe that children's work with ICT should be as continuous as possible throughout their school career. During Years 6, 7 and 8, and including both feeder and secondary schools, pupils could use similar software such as a CD-ROM encyclopedia and know that there are very similar policies in place with regard to use of the internet. These transition years offer an opportunity for looking again at how we design the curriculum; for example the inclusion of visual literacy may be an appropriate way of updating the curriculum. Since most countries have an institutional break during their children's education, although the timing may vary, we need to consider useful strategies for dealing with this in terms of increasing literacy demands. One such strategy might be the use of online language coaches.

Sue Brindley takes a long and considered view of how 'literacy' is evolving within educational contexts. She believes that many people already think of 'literacies' rather than 'literacy', and therefore we need to consider literacy as multi-dimensional. The current framework for Key Stage 3 literacy has been placed in the school subject of English and she claims the document gives every indication that the acquisition of literacy skills belongs primarily to a print-based medium.

Now that we have ICT, Brindley thinks it is time to consider where literacy belongs. Unfortunately, teachers have not been encouraged to explore the potential of literacies in their own subjects. How literacy is defined in education is partly controlled by those responsible for monitoring the curriculum, but ICT figures either not at all or marginally in monitored literacy requirements. So, we end up with what has been described by Margaret Meek as 'schooled literacy'. Surely we need to have 'shrewd and fluent readers' in technological contexts as well as more traditional contexts? She considers it is essential to critically understand how language and image can be used to persuade, manipulate and, on occasions, indoctrinate: 'To read against the text so that we are able better to understand its intentions.' Education will find it belongs in multi-dimensional literacy.

Geoff Barton in Chapter 3 explores current conceptions of English as a school subject and the liberating possibilities of ICT to help us redefine the essential ingredients of the subject. The government is trying to upgrade the literacy of the workforce and we need to know what our students are learning and whether or not we need to recast the essentials of English. He asks how far English should be about transmission of culture: should media form the new subject core and, indeed, how far can content be prescribed?

He claims English teachers are traditionally introspective and often their role is imbued with special responsiblilities as regards transmission of 'culture' and values. There has been little change in literacy levels for over 50 years, yet we do not do well in international comparisons. However, the framework for teaching literacy in secondary schools has introduced a new methodology.

Barton believes we must uphold our commitment to introducing and revealing to students our heritage of imaginative literature. However, the definition of English should shift away from what English teachers want to teach and move towards the skills and experiences our students need. English must help prepare students for the worlds of work and citizenship. Future students will need of course to be literate, but their literacy requirements will include visual literacy and language skills such as reading critically as well as using creative and precise expression. ICT is both a mode of learning and part of our teaching methodology which is transforming our world and so should transform our teaching and students' learning. Metacognition, the language of learning, should be central to the way we interact with students. Currently, English teachers need to be accomplished and up to date with research about learning, pedagogy and ICT. As he states, learning is bursting out of the artificial confines of the school day.

Chapter 4 focuses on practical examples of projects in secondary schools. Alison Tyldesley and Chris Turner believe that ICT has contributed to three key principles of teaching and learning by supporting good practice in subject teaching, by a direct relationship between the use of ICT and teaching and learning objectives and by using ICT to achieve something that could not have been achieved without its use. Their first case study involved the use of an interactive whiteboard to help those who had fallen behind in their literacy skills. The use of ICT improved the status of these units, so that students were much more willing to attend them. The use of ICT in the second case study occurred in lessons designed to improve students' argumentative styles of writing and included use of a CD-ROM encyclopedia. The passage used for comprehension was not decontextualized, it involved links to other pages so students had to choose which links to follow and also had to scroll up and down the screen, important reading skills for coping with digital texts. Literacy work with persuasive texts and the preparation of a presentation were linked in the third project. The literacy coordinator listed the advantages of using ICT to promote oracy and literacy: scaffolding, added realism, work-related relevance and potential for a professional end product. The students were very enthusiastic about the integration of ICT into this project. The fourth study incorporated the use of Powerpoint presentation software to create texts and bring about an interchange of these between an English and a Mexican school. The students in both countries were extremely motivated by the idea of the project and the means of developing it, particularly the motivational effect of designing texts for a definite audience. The literacy strategy asks teachers to explore new texts with pupils. Also pupils need to show that they understand textual features and linguistic choices by creating their own texts. Case study five concerns the use of computer-generated simulations. The authors conclude that ICT contributes something distinctive to literacy.

Aisha Walker and Rachel Pilkington in Chapter 5 begin from the premise that literacy may be defined as the set of skills needed to process information effectively using the communications media and languages of a given culture. Some students may have a 'literacy deficit' in which reading comprehension and written communication skills may lag behind other skills. Walker and Pilkington wished to find out if text-based computer-mediated communication (CMC) could enhance the literacy skills of lower secondary school children and help scaffold their development of written argument. They also aimed to look at the relationship between self-esteem, writing task and the quality of writing and see if they could offer any practical suggestions for supporting tutors. Previously, they had found research evidence that collaboration in writing is effective when authors engage in 'substantive conflict', that is, arguing alternative points of view.

After the project Walker and Pilkington decided that CMC can provide a setting for 'exploratory talk' and 'substantive conflict'. Over time, the pupils' turns increased in length and complexity. This alone suggests an increased fluency and confidence in writing. As sessions progressed, there was also a trend towards fewer, longer and more thoughtful turns, often revealing a shift from knowledge telling to knowledge transformation. There was less off-topic talk and pupils gave more reasons to support their views. Pupils became more inclusive in their remarks and less insulting or offensive. As the project continued, the pupils selected topics that prompted more debate, addressed each other's comments more, supported their opinions with more detailed arguments, engaged in more substantive conflict and debated points of disagreement. They had learned to pay attention to others' opinions and to see matters from other points of view. Spelling improved as children wanted to make their writing understandable, thus showing an awareness of audience. The teacher made more contributions online in later sessions (as he became less involved in trouble-shooting) and this may have encouraged the students online.

This significant chapter centres around the belief shared by Charles Crook and Roy Dymott that neither ICT nor writing has a singular identity. Indeed, writing is a rich system of activities and can be characterized as a cultural practice. They draw on an analogy with hunting. Guns arrive therefore hunting is different; ICT arrives therefore writing is different. Their example is taken from a body of undergraduate work and reveals clearly how such writing is an activity system. In many ways, this body of writing is similar to the coursework achieved by secondary students during their school years. Technology has always contributed dynamically to literacy practice; nowadays ICT reconfigures the way we manage document access and necessitates changes in interaction with the immediate writing environment. A large number of resources are available at one site on a PC: email, synchronous chat, TV, internet as well as word processing (or whatever program is in use). Crook and Dymott consider that use of the 'versatile' PC has encouraged what they call an 'animated' style of writing. In their research they found that students changed focus every four minutes or so, often for a recreational variation. This form of technology can 'socialise the writing process' so literacy itself becomes more social. This 'social' quality of literacy is noted again in Chapters 7 and 8.

As Crook and Dymott state, ICT offers a technology for making learner activity visible within the community of the classroom. Local websites such as school or university intranets make material from the learners themselves visible. Use of ICT can create common knowledge in the classroom, create an authentic sense of audience among novice writers and resource future learners. One student class could pass material to the next cohort or class. Writing for others is important to cultivate yet most student writing is not read by many people (probably only by the teacher). ICT in the form of web-based publishing offers considerable prospects for this sense of socialized literacy.

The last three chapters consider the relationship between ICT use outside school and what students do in school. The authors look at what teenagers actually write and read online, firstly, with a group of male pupils engaged with computer games and then a group of girls and their use of chatrooms. The final chapter focuses on a survey of internet use and the literacy skills involved.

Chapter 7 examines computer games as one example of a new literacy, a form from which Noel Williams believes students may learn useful practices. Educational concepts of literacy need adaptation to better reflect digital practice, as evidenced by the adept adolescent. As he says, literacy has never been a constant. It now includes an emphasis on purpose, audience and writing as a process. Reading is increasingly an intertextual phenomenon, while the internet requires information-retrieval skills, social communicative skills and evaluative skills. A shift from document as knowledge to document as resource means that ICT users must construct knowledge themselves. Reading on the internet requires evaluation as well as comprehension, writing requires a sense of audience plus a sense of their ephemeral contact 'with your' information.

Computer games are a medium which can encourage such digital skills. There is a stereotype of the computer gamer, often a misrepresentation, as a loner. Modern computer games involve players in communicative networks where new verbal skills are required and existing ones developed. Digital literacy is application-independent. An exploration of teenage literacy should examine whether ICT skills may (a) dilute or distract from traditional concepts of forms of literacy; (b) ICT skills can transfer to traditional skills of literacy and oracy; or (c) transform them.

His chapter is a microstudy of a small group of male adolescent computer gamers, six in all. Their gaming extends beyond computers to other forms of popular culture via action films, card games, comic books, war games. Internet Relay Chat (IRC) may liberate learners who find conventional or traditional communicative modes artificial, irrelevant or unsatisfying, but it is not merely a case of abandoning all constraints in order to speed up communication. Game players develop a sense of genre and narrative and even ask for help with grammar occasionally. Narrative structure is one component of game play, a major factor in player satisfaction.

Fanfiction websites exist, exhibiting examples of collaborative writing which would not exist without computer games. In using computer games, at least some adolescents exhibit traditional literacy skills, and also acquire intertextual skills. As digital literacy becomes increasingly social, students acquire modes of literacy possibly more relevant to future communicative needs than traditional print-based modes.

Guy Merchant also looks at IRC (internet relay chat), this time with a group of female teenagers. He agrees with Williams that young people move in a new electronic genre largely ignored in educational circles. A chatroom, a form of synchronous computer-mediated communication, requires a basic working knowledge of ICT, confident keyboard skills and involves quite specific kinds of literacy. IRC blurs distinctions between speech and writing and constitutes a new and developing linguistic form. Writing is used to do conversational work, so users resort to iconic and symbolic conventions for indicating seriousness, emphasis, surprise and so on. Message content becomes more important than surface polish because replies are needed quickly. The identity of participants is uncertain.

Quite specific linguistic features are being developed to substitute for paralinguistic and prosodic features, actions and gestures. The author noticed vowel reduplication, expletives, non-standard punctuation, capitalization, abbreviations and use of emoticons. (Some of these features are discussed in Chapter 5.) Merchant notes roughly four types of cate-gorizations: non-alphabetic characters, such as emoticons; initial letters as shorthand, such as LOL, laughing out loud; combinations of letters and numbers to create an approximate phonetic rendering of a message, for example NE1 for anyone; and phonetic spelling, such as wot. Usually chat-users found out about these uses by experience online, occasionally from games magazines or ordinary teenage magazines. They also regularly transferred language features between different media – song lyrics, adverts, TV, magazines, text messages, across the whole field of popular culture.

Young people are active agents in a developing linguistic market. Although they are criticized for their 'aberrant use of language' they are developing 'marketable skills, which may become capital' in a new technologized social order. The field of new communication is a site in which a complex struggle for domination is in progress. The forces of an emergent global culture, supported by commercial interests, are pitted against more conservative forces of the education system and other agents of language control.

There are moves to reinstate formal grammar in the school curriculum. There is a tension to be resolved between a traditional view of language and the need to respond to social and economic change. Despite political encouragement to develop the use of new technology in the classroom, educational thinking about ICT is plagued by contradiction. We are reluctant to value the skills and knowledge that pupils develop outside the classroom. Rather than drawing on young people's experience, we problematize popular forms. Now we have a generational digital divide we need a more creative response to popular forms.

The book concludes with a survey of how parents and children are using the internet. This chapter is particularly relevant as we have recently become more aware of what is out there on the net, much of which teachers would not consider as 'educational'. The problems of censorship and the necessity for full discussion of what is on the internet are recent developments. This knowledge does herald a new awareness, where the benefits and abuses of literacy are both clearly available. Since this is a new and rather startling result of continuing trends, we have given this last chapter an individual introduction.

Kwok-Wing Lai states that the concept of literacy has to be redefined to include skills of accessing, processing and evaluating information gathered from the internet. Literacy is now about the skills that young people need in order to function in the information society. They need to know about illegal use of the internet and about material which is inappropriate for their age or unacceptable on ethical grounds. Parents need to know about youth culture and the inherent risks connected with use of the internet. Kwok-Wing Lai's research about email use found that it was mainly social, although a minority of pupils used it extensively for school. Only a small proportion appeared to have come across unsuitable material, and only a minority thought there were any risks in using email and the web. However, some students divulged personal information to strangers even during the first communicative occasion.

Parents in this survey were unaware of the risks involved, though they were aware of their responsibilities with regard to internet use at home. However, they thought the use of the internet to be similar to uses of other media. The majority of both parents and students believed that some censorship of access to the internet was necessary. The most general example used was physical supervision. Some parents encouraged discussion of specific and undesirable sites, in order to damp down curiosity. Often parents checked on the actual sites visited. Both parents and students were fairly comfortable with the degree of censorship imposed at home. Parents were perhaps overconfident as the pupils reported little supervision at home, compared with that at school. Parents had little knowledge of how or to whom their children sent email at school. Therefore they could not use collaborative strategies joining with other parents or schoolteachers concerned with censorship. These parents were often highly ICT literate, but the evidence reinforces the notion of a 'digital divide' between generations as mentioned in Chapters 7 and 8. Kwok-Wing Lai believes we must move towards a critical media literacy which includes skills and tools young people have to acquire so that they can evaluate text, sound and images that are readily accessible from the internet.

These last three chapters surely indicate that we as teachers should encourage more use of CMC in the classroom. This is particularly relevant given the positive findings in Chapter 5. It is important that we stress the value of literacy as well as the itemized steps in our literacy curriculum. We need more discussion in school about the kinds of literacy involved both in traditional schooling and online. It is impossible to underestimate the desire of most people to become literate. Currently in the world there are still many people like Chico Mendes who desperately wished to learn how to be literate (Mendes 1989). Still illiterate at 18 on a 'rubber estate in the Amazon' he had to walk for three hours along a narrow trail in the forest each weekend after work to meet with a man prepared to teach him how to read and write. As they had no text book, they used newspapers that were a month or two old by the time they reached them. Even under those circumstances, he learned in a year.

As developing countries push up their numbers of literate people, they will inevitably come across new digital communications and will also have to consider the wider implications of literacy in a digital age. We may well need to worry about the seepage of 'NE1' and similar verbalizations across media, but there is hardly any point in banning them outright without discussion. The skills of discrimation, evaluation, and a sense of appropriate context and audience are as essential to literacy in the secondary stages of education as they always have been. However, as teachers we need to collaborate with our students in the production of new literacy forms and simultaneously develop guidelines as to their general application.

References

Braggins, J. (2001) *Shared Responsibilities: Education for Prisoners at a Time of Change.* London: NATFHE.

Colquhoun, S. (2002) *The Lecturer,* July, p. 3. London: NATFHE.

Department for Education and Employment (DfEE) (1999a) *A Fresh Start: Improving Literacy and Numeracy,* the report of the working group chaired by Sir Claus Moser. London: HMSO.

Department for Education and Employment (DfEE) (1999b) *National Literary Strategy: Review of Research and Other Related Evidence.* www.standards.dfee.gov.uk/library/research/b5/policy/lit

Department of Education and Science (DES) (1975) *A Language for Life,* the report of the Committee of Inquiry under the Chairmanship of Sir Alan Bullock FBA. London: HMSO.

Hafner, S. (2002) *International Herald Tribune,* 21 September.

Hughes, L. (2002) Letter to the *Guardian* newspaper, 15 August.

Lee, J. (2002) *International Herald Tribune,* 21 September.

Literacy Trust (2002a) www.literacytrust.org.uk/about/OECDrelease.html

Literacy Trust (2002b) www.literacytrust.org.uk/about/vitallink.html

Mendes, C. (1989) *Fight for the Forest.* London: Latin American Bureau.

THE POSITION OF LITERACY WITHIN THE SECONDARY CURRICULUM

Moira Monteith and Sarah Monteith

Now that literacy in the sense of 'becoming literate' is not seen as belonging only in the primary school, the debate has widened to include the secondary school. New points feature as the discussion continues, including that of the apparent mismatch between primary and secondary teaching and learning. This chapter looks at the context of literacy in the secondary school, how far some schemes and initiatives benefit students and whether or not Information Communication Technology (ICT) is a positive factor in becoming and continuing to be literate.

What people wish to say seems to remain remarkably constant across the ages, yet the forms of literacy alter. Humans have used different implements over time to make marks on materials ranging from papyrus to parchment, stone, wood, wax, slate, paper and so on. ICT is now the latest literacy technology. It is a medium on which or through which we write and it also presents us with the widest range of reading material yet available. It seems likely that most, if not all, changes to writing and reading systems have occurred as a result of technological inventions. Consequently, it seems only sensible that we use ICT (among other more traditional literacy technologies) to boost or maintain literacy levels in schools.

There are three points in particular which feature in discussions concerning literacy in post-primary education. First, there is an economic argument. Employers in 1890 or thereabouts told local headteachers boys needed only to be able to read and write, nothing more (or less), before they came to work in factories. These employers knew a literate workforce would benefit industries which were becoming much more organized affairs where workers were expected to clock in and out, there were penalties for lateness, and various sets of instructions (including those about safety) had to be read. Nowadays the argument is often configured as a deficiency model: we lose millions of pounds through a workforce where certain people are not employable in certain job vacancies (Geoff Barton makes the point more fully in Chapter 3). Or, so the financial argument goes, they move towards joining a criminal underclass who then cost us millions of pounds via the prison system. The argument about employability does make sense. Certainly, in modern workplaces it is difficult to imagine anyone working today who won't be using ICT at some stage of their working life. Workers need to be both literate and literate with ICT.

Second there is an argument revolving around citizenship. Citizens need to have some basic literacy to vote in the UK in that they must know their names are on the current voting list, they then have to read candidates' names on a ballot paper or voting slip and put a cross against one. Of course, citizenship implies a wider set of skills than merely those used in the mechanics of voting and wider citizenship skills necessarily involve people being articulate. The first time language skills were linked officially with citizenship and democracy was in the *Kingman Report*. Subsequently the first edition of the *National Curriculum for English* document quoted a section from the Kingman Report:

> People need expertise in language to be able to participate effectively in a democracy. There is no point in having access to information that you cannot understand . . . A democratic society needs people who have the linguistic abilities which will enable them to discuss, evaluate and make sense of what they are told, as well as to take effective action on the basis of their understanding . . . Otherwise there can be no genuine participation, but only the imposition of the ideas of those who are linguistically capable.
>
> Kingman Report, Chapter 2, paragraph 2, as cited in
> *The National Curriculum: English for Ages 5 to 11* (DES 1988)

Citizenship is now a subject on the secondary curriculum. The continuing development of a civic society and the values which uphold such a society must involve a literate citizenry. Moreover, it seems that people's perceived inclusion in society often has a strong base in their level of literacy.

There is also the argument concerning levels of education. Can an 'educated' person be considered fully articulate if they cannot read or write very well? Indeed, we perhaps need other literacy skills, such as those belonging in the area of visual literacy and other 'new' literacies. These three points or arguments indicate that literacy goals in secondary schools are bound to be different from those prevailing in the primary phase of schooling where pupils are encouraged to read and write as ends in themselves. This is not to undervalue the wider context of teaching and learning that happens in primary school merely to indicate that the final goals are different. Literacy for older pupils involves a complex of skills from filling in forms, reading instructions on frozen food packets to being able to use the alphabet as a sorting strategy as well as writing poetry and many other activities they began in primary classes. ICT has brought other literacy requirements and possibilities such as texting messages, sending graphics alongside or embedded within email messages, changing and editing documents, reading online and creating websites.

Break in continuity

When the National Curriculum came into being in 1988 it encouraged a holistic view of state education. It proposed a curriculum which ran straight through from years 1 to 11 (pupils aged from 5 to 16). However, in the UK we have a historic break in state education at the age of 11. This break became general after 1944 when pupils went to different schools: grammar, technical and secondary modern. Before that a minority of children went to grammar schools and the majority stayed where they were in elementary schools. This division between primary and secondary appears to matter scholastically. Anecdotal accounts exist of children who begin to learn one modern language such as French in primary school and then have to learn Spanish or German in the secondary school. Similarly, there are accounts about children who have worked effectively and well with ICT in the primary school which they attended and then use it hardly at all in the first couple of years at secondary level. Some individuals suffer. For example, one boy with learning difficulties who was greatly helped by the use of a laptop in primary school (Jones 2001) was unable to have such support in the secondary school because the laptop couldn't move schools with him.

There is also the widespread difficulty that different sets of institutions often distrust the learning experiences within other educational establishments. Such a difficulty appears to exist concerning perceptions of learning between higher education and schools and colleges as well as between secondary and primary schools. Any changeover is highly contextualized and may or may not relate to problems with literacy. At the age of 11, pupils move from a situation where they are the 'senior' class in the school to another institution where they are the youngest and often deemed the least capable of classes. They go from having the 'parent' figure of one class teacher on whom they depend for virtually all learning to moving between 10 to 15 teachers, all with different expectations. In addition, almost each subject requires a different form of literacy. Significantly, in secondary schools there is no counterpart to early years teachers in primary schools who add so much value to learning capacity and development.

The Literacy Trust website (www.literacytrust.org) has included various items of evidence that literacy gains go down in some secondary schools in . . . the first months of the changeover: '40 per cent of pupils lose motivation and make no progress in the year after transfer . . . The situation is very similar throughout the UK' (*TES*, 21 June 2002). The website also included comments from Ofsted's chief inspector David Bell who stated that primary school gains can too often be lost at transfer and described it as 'a long-standing weakness in the English state school system'. David Miliband, government schools' minister, said that the transition was still too often marred by lack of data, different teaching styles, failure to build on progress, and differing expectations between primary and secondary schools.

Nor does the situation appear only in English schools. Susan Lewis, Wales' chief inspector has stated that standards in Welsh primary schools have been rising so fast that some 9-year-old pupils were more literate and numerate than their 15-year-old counterparts. Ms Lewis declared that higher standards especially at Key Stage 1 reflected the effort schools were putting in to the national literacy drive. However, as in England, standards have been found to dip in the early secondary years, especially between the ages of 12 and 14. The weakest teaching appeared in Year 8 and was unsatisfactory in a tenth of all classes.

The situation is not so simple as it might appear, either in Wales or in England. Other features of the debate are beginning to surface. In Wales differences exist between the various schools and the languages they use for learning and teaching. Bilingualism in itself is a positive factor in terms of language use (Bruck and Genesee 1994) and possibly has been a factor contributing to overall excellence in literacy in Welsh schools. However, there are differences in literacy attainment between schools of differently organized pupil groups, for example those with primarily Welsh speakers, those with primarily English speakers, those taught in Welsh or English or a mixture of any of the above factors (Evans 2002). This indicates just how complicated the situation is when we consider language use and general educational development.

When we examine how we test literacy we can see that the testing itself throws up problems. If we look carefully at the report from the Qualifications and Curriculum Authority (QCA) we can see the complexity of the issues. (www.qca.org.uk/rs/rer/ks3_report.asp)

There were two research studies on the effects of the school transition which covering years 4 to 10, investigated pupils' ability to demonstrate and use a range of literacy skills. In all of the areas investigated the average test performance of boys and girls showed some signs of going back or at least of standing still. In general, the dip seems temporary, however, and most pupils appear to be back on track by year 10.

Different aspects of literacy were considered. In reading, 'there is evidence of a dip in the levels of performance around year 7 or year 8'. In spelling, 'performance again dipped, or at least the improvement slowed down, in every task'. With regard to use of punctuation 'another consistent picture emerges: the effect is always greatest for the lower ability pupils'. As regards writing, 'more able pupils do not seem even to experience difficulty; their writing ability continues to develop without pause.' The report adds: 'It is important to recognise that this [writing] task was a complex piece of composition where pupils had to address a specific audience, in order to achieve a particular purpose.'

To summarize, boys and girls in years 7 and 8 seem to have lost some of the ability they had in years 5 and 6 to handle language accurately. Where tasks are more complex and involve longer texts, the pattern of results suggests that less able pupils do not make progress or indeed regress. In more tightly structured tasks focusing on single aspects, the majority of pupils show some slowing of progress. This is more marked for the less able. This may be significant for pupils at this point faced with substantial new cognitive demands in years 7 and 8, demands that the less able find difficult. The more able pupils are able to cope with this new demand without losing much control over the mechanics of language. They do show signs of difficulty with grammar, reading and writing, when they attend to texts in their entirety. Less able pupils find the demands too much for them; in order to cope with whole tasks and whole texts they seem to switch their capacity away from the details.

Nevertheless, the report takes a reasonably optimistic view. It asks if perhaps pupils are moving 'from learning language to learning to use language? . . . The appearance of increased inaccuracy may paradoxically be a sign that pupils are learning to tackle the challenges of using language for new purposes. The apparent regression may in fact be a sign of progress.' It seems that instead of 'gradually mastering each feature of grammar or spelling in turn . . . pupils make pretty much the same sorts of errors in year 9 as they did in year 5, they just make them less often'. The report affirms: 'the curious dip in performance seen around years 7 and 8 may be seen as evidence of change and of progress' even though a set of questions challenges any complacency:

• Do Key Stage 2 pupils perform so well partly because they are not set a sufficient range of challenging tasks?
• Should early Key Stage 3 pupils be given more help in adjusting to the new demands of using language for many different purposes?

- Would this particularly help the lowest 25 per cent to deal with complexity?
- Should Key Stage 3 teachers pay more attention to helping children apply their literacy skills in the context of new cognitive demands?
- Should Key Stage 3 teachers ignore the problem because pupils generally recover from the dip?

The report admits that the research 'focused on aspects of English that can be most easily described and assessed'. It is difficult to test complex matters of language use so we need to remember this research involved a precise and rather narrow view of literacy. It is possible that more sophisticated tests will be developed in future. Meanwhile it does seem clear that the transition from one school to another can be problematic.

Use of ICT to help during transition

Given the nature of the difficulties outlined above, one of the questions we ask in this chapter is whether or not ICT could help across the transfer from primary to secondary school. As in the numeracy and literacy strategies, ICT runs across the curriculum and can therefore assist with literacy work in any subject area. ICT can change boundaries not by changing subject areas but helpfully organizing support across them. Data, how we use it and how it is transformed into knowledge is one of the most important cross-curricular building blocks. With that in mind, use of ICT is ideally suited to assist with changes involving the 'new cognitive demands' indicated in the QCA Report.

Research findings on exploratory talk

Research projects considering specific aspects of ICT in education often have important insights for education as a whole. The original SLANT (Spoken Language and New Technology) project was established to look at the nature of group conversation among children round a computer. Many teachers had commented that they found group discussion around a computer was one of the best uses of ICT in the classroom. However, SLANT researchers found that often the pupils' talk was off the point, or very abrupt with monosyllabic answers and very little discussion (Wegerif and Dawes 2000). A research team from the Open University working with practising teachers in their own classrooms developed approaches to learning using 'exploratory talk'. Neil Mercer claims that in such talk 'Knowledge is made accountable and reasoning is visible in the talk' (Mercer 2000). He further states that such talk 'is a way of using language for thinking together which is valued highly in most societies – it embodies the principles of accountability, of clarity, of constructive criticism and receptiveness to well-argued proposals.'

Exploratory talk in these projects was introduced and promoted through teachers and students agreeing on a set of ground rules for use in discussion. These rules tend to focus on the following points, though each class negotiates and agrees its own set of rules:

1. We share our ideas and listen to each other
2. We talk one at a time
3. We respect each other's opinions
4. We give reasons to explain our ideas
5. If we disagree we ask 'why?'
6. We try to agree in the end.

(Mercer 2000)

Later research in classrooms using software which helped promote discussion on moral issues found that pupils who had been encouraged and shown how to use 'exploratory talk' solved puzzles more successfully than those who did not use such talk in group projects. 'But a more surprising finding was that the . . . children also got significantly better at doing the . . . test *on their own*. It was as if they were internalizing the kinds of joint reasoning they had been involved in – and then recreating it in their own heads.' Not only was this research happening in what might be termed 'ordinary' schools and not in laboratory conditions, the positive findings were repeated in the SATS scores, tests all the schools take rather than tests geared to examine aspects for particular research. The results indicate a transfer of learning which is both exciting and encouraging (see www.thinkingtogether.org.uk). These findings should alert us also to the fact that ICT use itself is embedded within a learning context and we always need to consider the whole context.

Policy making across the transition

Agreeing sets of rules such as the ground rules described above obviously builds on a very common human activity. The Opies witnessed children ostensibly playing games but actually spending a great deal of the time discussing rules and who should do what (Opie 1959). As we all know, people continuously discuss game rules from Dungeons and Dragons to football. And, of course, there is always bureaucracy which continues to expand with a multiplicity of rules. Agreeing ground rules doubtless would benefit other education areas as well as those concerned with exploratory talk. In addition, being explicit about ICT use in students' learning can ʾoth teachers and students consider the issue of thinking skills and metacognition could take place.

The policy documents teachers have to compile and update are a form of rule making. Requests for examples of policies on all subjects are frequently placed on teachers' online conferences. Other teachers who reply to these requests recommend websites such as www.icteachers.co.uk because many examples of policy documents can be found there. In fact, the easiest thing may be to start with one such policy as a first draft. The word 'policies' gives the impression perhaps that practice might be bound in concrete, but surely agreed rules for ICT use across the transition would have very positive outcomes. There are two obvious needs to be addressed: pupil use of ICT in school certainly shouldn't diminish between years 6 and 7 or 8; secondly, students could be introduced to a common policy with regard to use of the internet over those years of schooling. Other 'ground rules' could be discussed and agreed by the particular schools involved with transition classes, including use of similar software and gradual development of generic ICT skills such as use of databases.

Data across the curriculum

Teachers rightly list a number of problems involved with searching for information: for example, unfocused work, the downloading of texts with a level of difficulty in comprehension beyond that of the students' current level, or students visiting undesirable websites. However, looking at all kinds of data can generate a great deal of on-task discussion and reading this information can be of considerable help in terms of literacy, by focusing on non-fiction texts.

Pupils may need to be taught specific skills if they have not learned them already but many pupils will be well aware of web searches, either from home use or from their previous school. Each school needs proposals as to how this combination of skills may be managed. Open discussion with pupils about web use will be helpful in initiating rules which will need updating regularly. Clearly pupils must enter or accept an agreement whereby they do not spend time surfing the web on topics away from the one agreed. (Although it is true, serendipitous finds do sometimes occur.) It is very important that schools do discuss internet use for every subject area. It might also be possible and efficient for students to download material for several lessons in one time-tabled period, provided that this is an agreed procedure.

Required information or data can be looked for in CD-ROM encyclopedias. These have the benefit of being generally available via school libraries and can be used for a number of subject areas. Also, the level of prose difficulty can be established more effectively than with a variety of texts downloaded from the internet. Therefore it would be helpful if schools knew which non-fiction CD-ROMS were used by other local schools across the transition. Search strategies and the procedures undertaken by staff and pupils in gaining appropriate data might also be agreed. For example, during the last six months in primary and first six months in secondary schools pupils could use the same or similar encyclopedias or other non-fiction works and with agreed searching strategies. Turning information gathering into knowledge is a further stage but can be widely assisted by agreed procedures.

Surfing across the curriculum

Once the school has a working procedure on internet policy in place it should be comparatively easy to continue with the necessary spot checks every now and then. Preparation time is very important for web searches and can be accomplished away from computers. Tatiana Wilson (Wilson 2002) has shown how effective 'knowledge grids' can be. She developed a grid partly based on the exit model developed by Wray and Lewis and already used by teachers as it was included in the National Literacy Strategy documentation on 'Reading and Writing for information.' She combined this with the KWL grid where K = what I know, W = what I want to know, and L = what I have learned. This also keeps an account of what the children have learned for future use. She finally came up with the headings:

What I know	What I want to find out	Search words (Using +" "or ñ)	What I learnt	Where I found the information (websites)

Pupils can usefully spend time developing questions for a search, before actually looking for the information. Wilson suggests using discussion strategies for developing appropriate questions.

Of course, some contradictory situations can arise. For example, sites, which are considered educationally positive such as BBC education web-pages, can be blocked to pupils because of some information on particular websites at a given time. In a particular case described by Wilson it was information on abuses in slavery which were detailed on the website and these were topics excluded by the school online barriers. However, as Wilson discovered, able pupils with persistent searches can circumvent such barriers anyway. In most schools now, teachers can over-ride such website problems by downloading in advance the relevant pages on to their school intranet.

ICT gives a purpose and an audience for writing

Material in the form of letters, stories and written work on a range of topics including science and geography can be put up on a school website or exchanged with other schools, locally, nationally and internationally. Challenging areas in subjects such as citizenship, PSHE and inter-pretations of historical events can be discussed online in the school via computer conferencing software or talk sites on the school intranet. Sub-sequently a school point of view can be sent to various young people's discussion groups via the internet. Numerous legitimate websites exist for this purpose. Schools can exchange such work, particularly across years 6 to 8, from primary to secondary and vice versa. This would enable more demanding topics to be introduced in year 6 and continued and developed in years 7 and 8.

As Crook and Dymott point out in Chapter 6, often the fate of students' written work is that it will be read only by the teacher. The use of more public audiences could be highly significant in raising the level of literacy awareness and quite possibly of individual literacy abilities as well.

New literacies

There is no general agreement as to how many new kinds of literacy there are. Even if we accept that there is a consensus as to the existence of 'visual literacy', various definitions as to what that is co-exist. We are concerned with forms of written expression here which can include images, but not with the extension of meaning found in terms such as 'emotional literacy', 'political literacy' and so on. No doubt in the near future definition of visual literacy will be codified and generally accepted. Even when this happens, a case has to be made for its relevance with what children learn between the ages of 10 and 12. Some people may consider that visual literacy is really a matter for media studies and therefore left at least until the later years of secondary school. Others may consider we have enough on our plates trying to encourage pupils to become fully literate in the traditional sense without worrying about new versions of literacy. In fact, these years during which most pupils are changing from one school to another make a most appropriate time for re-considering the curriculum and what is happening to learning, particularly in terms of the com-bination of learning at home and at school. The expansion of what is considered as literacy may well be a case in point.

In some schools children begin very early to consider how stories can be presented visually. Jon Callow and Katrina Zammit (2002) give a descrip-tion as to what happens in some Australian schools where children at the age of six discuss how to make a wolf in a story look more fierce. The children decided that how close you are to the wolf makes a difference to its fierce appearance. They drew close-up pictures with pencils and pens and also took close-up photographs with a digital camera, comparing the two. In this class, the 'children were encouraged to read pictures and text, learning how to discuss and interpret not only the written meanings but the visual meanings as well'.

Since pupils in the last years at primary school and the first at secondary may well be using the same or similar encyclopedias or non-fiction texts such as 'How Things Work' on CD-ROM it is important to think about how pupils/students will deal with these new genres or at the least old genres in a new form. We can draw a valid comparison with the time when children consciously begin to use books. Marie Clay focused in her reading readiness research (Clay 1979) on the early learning that children acquire about books and print. They find out how to turn pages, how to follow print from one side of the page to another and from the top downwards and indeed to start at the beginning of a book, right side up. This is before they think of what they might be reading. Now children from a very early age look at texts on computer and TV screens; even books include words mixed in with images and text at different levels in different fonts. In addition, text is no longer contained within books only but on screens, clothes, equipment and walls everywhere.

As Callow and Zammit conclude:

> How to learn to learn is important in any learning environment be it paper-based or electronic. Given the range of texts that are part of a child's school we can not assume children can expertly read all the different forms. The use of visual and multimodal texts as resources within the classroom is going to increase and we need to provide children with opportunities to learn about, as well as from, these texts. Providing children with a language to talk about visual texts and engaging children in critiquing them can form the basis of the teaching and learning of multimodal texts.

Agreement between schools as to when and how children begin to critique multimodal texts can only be beneficial. It would ensure a constructive learning environment, introducing new concepts to children. This learning could be built on subsequently, throughout their secondary schooling.

Years 6 and 7

Some schools have developed schemes of work which run across the last terms of primary schooling to the first term in secondary. For instance, children begin reading a novel in primary school and finish it in the secondary. In the case of written work, they may complete a diary or journal, often arising from their reading about travels or explorations. If they compose it using ICT they could make a smooth transition from writing in one school to another. It is useful to try out such a project anyway. If the procedure is not smooth then clearly the ICT links between schools are not working appropriately and this signals that changes need to be made. Once the links are effective in terms of email and who receives what work then liaison between the schools will be that much more efficient. Children's work in ICT can be forwarded without difficulty, providing files are kept intact. It takes time to scan in other work but when completed is a compact archive which can be added to and moved with the pupil. This goes some way to meet the minister's complaint as to lack of data in terms of each pupil's achievements. Children could be encouraged to update some work to their own archived files.

Teachers, pupils and individual literacy

We have considered collaboration in learning and cooperative activities. As the exploratory talk results show, such cooperation often bears fruit in individual learning. However, parents and pupils may well be concerned with the level of success pupils are achieving in their individual literacy work.

It is obvious that as individuals we do not all learn skills in the same time-span or as speedily as each other. Nevertheless, almost every one of us learns to speak in a comparatively short time despite immense differences with regard to linguistic backgrounds. We have problems though in gaining universal literacy. Some schools use Integrated Learning Systems (ILS), for individual language work. Research indicates (Underwood 2002) that the most beneficial use of ILS depends upon its inclusion within the mainstream work of the classroom. If children are withdrawn from class for an hour or so by themselves or in a remedial grouping, the use of ILS is not so efficacious. The ILS system must have current status within the school, not be seen as something weaker students have to use. In addition, use of a closed system such as the ILS is not always useful or flexible enough when children's literacy is examined in a general context.

Use of external tutors can make a difference to the literacy level of individual pupils perhaps paralleling the way teachers make a difference when they are overseeing students' work on an ILS. The Southern Californian Writing Project (Marcus 1998) has pioneered work with writing coaches, often drawn from people outside the school system who each agree to help with one or two particular pupils. Email is definitely a useful link as students can email written work to their tutor for comment. Tutors must be vetted of course and understand what they are about but the system works well when it is in place. Often retired teachers or students in higher education who can include such coaching as an agreed unit of work provide excellent tuition and motivation.

Conclusion

Change is not always inimical and can be beneficial. Often, young people's literacy goes up when they get their first job and research has shown that 'people's literacy skills do alter after they leave school, improving into early middle age . . .' (A Fresh Start, DfEE 1999). So there is no irrefutable reason why pupils' standard change from one institution to another should mean a downsize in literacy levels. Use of ICT can help in the following ways:

• Policies in use of ICT can be developed across the transition by neighbouring schools.
• Strategies for collecting and sorting data could be agreed.
• Identical or very similar software could be used.
• Rules for use of the internet could be similar.
• Children's work could be archived and sent from one school to another.
• New areas such as visual literacy could be developed and introduced.
• Email links could be established so that continuous work could be maintained across the transition.
• Schools could establish email links with external language tutors.

References

Bruck, M. and Genesee, F. (1995) Phonological awareness in young second language learners, *Journal of Child Language*, 22: 307–24. Cambridge: Cambridge University Press.

Callow, J. and Zammit, K. (2002) Visual literacy: from picture books to electronic texts, in M. Monteith (ed.) *Teaching Primary Literacy with ICT*. Buckingham: Open University Press.

Clay, M. (1979) *The Early Detection of Reading Difficulties*. London: Heinemann.

Department for Education and Science (DES) (1988a) *Report of the Committee of Inquiry into the Teaching of the English Language* (Kingman Report). London: HMSO.

Department for Education and Science (DES) (1988b) *The National Curriculum: English for Ages 5 to 11*. London: HMSO.

Evans, G. (2002) Science advisory teacher for Cynnal (covering Gwynedd, Anglesey and Conwy LEAs). Unpublished report. Caernarfon, Gwynedd.

Jones, L. (2002) Transforming writing, *MAPE Newsletter*, Spring, p. 6. Birmingham: MAPE Publications.

Marcus, S. (2000) Picture information literacy, in M. Monteith (ed.) *IT for Learning Enhancement*, 2nd edn. Exeter: Intellect Books.

Mercer, N. (2000) *ICT and Interthinking*, occasional paper. Milton Keynes: Centre for Language and Communications, Open University.

Opie, I. and Opie, P. (1959) *The Lore and Language of School Children*. Oxford: Clarendon Press.

Qualifications and Curriculum Authority (QCA) (2002) Do pupils get steadily better at reading and writing English as they progress through school? Research and evaluation report. www.qca.org.uk/rs/rer/ks3_report.asp.

Underwood, J. (2002) Computer support for reading development, in M. Monteith (ed.) *Teaching Primary Literacy with ICT*. Buckingham: Open University Press.

Wegerif, R. and Dawes, L. (2000) Encouraging exploratory talk around computers, in M. Monteith (ed.) *IT for Learning Enhancement*, 2nd edn. Exeter: Intellect Books.

Wilson, T. (2002) Children, literacy and the world wide web, in M. Monteith (ed.) *Teaching Primary Literacy with ICT*. Buckingham: Open University Press.

2

ARE YOU SUN LITERATE? LITERACY, ICT AND EDUCATION POLICY IN THE UK: LITERACY – WHO DEFINES?

Sue Brindley

Where do you stand on the literacy spectrum? The ways in which you define literacy will, in their turn, define where and indeed if ICT has any part to play in your thinking about the relationship between the two.

The ends of the spectrum, though nowhere formally defined, might be represented as a working definition by two positionings: one a formal (though not statutory) document: the UK Key Stage Three National Strategy Framework for Teaching English; Years 7, 8 and 9 (KS3F), and the other a newspaper article on coping with the dangers of sunburn. The latter begins:

> We all like to think we're sun literate. And yet, on the first truly sunny lunchtime of summer, we head to the park to soak up a few golden rays. After all, a couple of hours isn't going to do any harm, is it?
> But this kind of misguided thinking is putting an increased number of us at risk. Figures released by Cancer Research UK . . .
> (The Sun Trap, *Style Magazine*, *Sunday Times*, 11 May 2003: 36)

At the other end of the spectrum and with more significance (for education anyway) the KS3F is clear that literacy is about 'raising standards' (9) and the means for doing this are outlined as a series of explicit skills to be acquired (with speaking and listening added on 'to support English teachers in planning to meet the full demands of the National Curriculum . . .': 10).

The KS3F states:

By the end of Year 9, we expect each pupil to be a shrewd and fluent independent reader:

- orchestrating a range of strategies to get at meaning in text
- sensitive to the way meanings are made
- reading in different ways for different purposes, including skimming to pick up quickly the gist of a text
- reflective, critical and discriminating in response to a wide range of printed and visual texts;

a confident writer:

- able to write for a variety of purposes and audiences
- able to write imaginatively, effectively and correctly
- able to shape, express, experiment with and manipulate sentences
- able to organize, develop, spell and punctuate writing accurately

an effective speaker and listener

- with the clarity and confidence to convey a point of view or information
- using talk to explore, create, question and revise ideas
- able to work effectively with others in a range of roles
- having a varied repertoire of styles, which are used appropriately

(KS3F: 10)

All of these skills, being carefully and painstakingly taught and, it is hoped, learned over the ten years of Key Stages 1, 2 and 3 through the National Literacy Strategy and then the KS3F are seen, as the Rationale (9) explains: 'the key to raising standards across all subjects, and equipping pupils with the skills and knowledge they need for life beyond school' (KS3F: 9).

If you are still wondering where you stand between sun literacy and KS3F literacy, there is a median point: they both refer to understanding – one of the impact of sun on us, and the other, impact of language. And both have the intention of equipping us with dealing with 'life beyond school' and life in the millennium: greater attention to the impact of the sun is because of events related to recent environmental changes; greater attention to language as literacy is because of the need to produce individuals working in the context of world economies.

So far, so good. We can see we need to protect ourselves from various twenty-first-century dangers. But this is where the two representations diverge. Sun literacy asks us to place ourselves clearly in a world we have come to see as needing differing understandings – sun is no longer simply good for a tan: it needs to be understood in a new context. The question I want to ask is should literacy also be understood in a new context – and specifically whether the KS3F can be seen as adequate in a world where, as David Puttnam states:

> Literacy is not . . . [a] simple thing . . . If being literate is best understood as being fully operational in the society in which we are found, then our notion of what literacy is, is likely to change along with that society. When the only requirement was to read the odd signpost just sounding out letters was probably fine, but when we are expected to digest the full flow of written and pictorial information that the internet provides we need to be equipped with a significantly higher order of skills. Our notion of what it is to be fully prepared for life has grown to encompass skills other than 'just reading'.
>
> (Puttnam 2001)

So who defines literacy (1)?

This is not a chapter which seeks to argue for the concept of literacies. That case has been effectively argued and long been made. So it is taken here as axiomatic that we acknowledge the need to see literacy as multi-dimensional. The case we are exploring here is how far government policies on teaching literacy have recognized that the need to teach *literacies* exists, and what this recognition looks like in policy documents and whose responsibility it is to enact the policy requirements of teaching literacies.

It is true that the KS3F acknowledges an ICT literacy need. In the reading section, it states that readers need to be reflective, critical and discriminating in response to a wide range of printed and visual texts. This is simultaneously heartening and curious. In a document which makes little acknowledgement of the notion that literacy exists beyond a skills acquisition model, the inclusion of the phrase 'visual texts', tantalizing in its inclusion and disappointing in its lack of expansion, raises the question of whether 'transferable sustainable skills' are as watertight as they seem.

However, from my own perspective as an English teacher, this is a document replete with tensions and contradictions. It states clearly and unequivocally that literacy is the responsibility of all teachers: 'language is the prime medium through which pupils learn and express themselves across the curriculum, and all teachers have a stake in effective literacy' (KS3F: 10) and the theme of cross-curricular responsibility is developed at length in the eponymous section Literacy Across the Curriculum: 'The best practice is seen in schools where all departments plan systematically to address language issues related to the subject . . .' (KS3F: 10).

But the document is called not, as we might expect, the Key Stage 3

Framework for literacy, but *for teaching English*. Much of the text is aimed at English teachers and indeed, in the section entitled Progression, it states: 'Progression in English has different dimensions' thus conflating English and literacy almost as a positional statement. This has implication for English teachers, of course, and Chris Davies' *What is English Teaching* (1996) addresses most effectively the problems raised by such a position, seen over a number of initiatives including the ill-fated *Language Across the Curriculum*.

But there are other and perhaps more immediate problems with this position. By labelling literacy as English, all other subject teachers are made to feel marginalized in the teaching of literacy, if not completely excluded. The responsibility is elsewhere – with the English department. This seems to me to be a fundamentally flawed position. If we do indeed want shrewd and fluent readers and confident writers (and who would question that?) that surely should be the concern of all educators. The KS3F manages both to espouse that position and deny it.

However, let us move forward on this point and simply agree that the KS3F is concerned with literacy for all, by all. What is meant by literacy in this document?

In the KS3F version of literacy, print reading and writing are prioritized as pre-requisites for all other literacies, and the KS3F gives the context of acquiring these skills as an almost ICT-free environment. The acquisition of literacy skills belongs primarily to a print based medium and once these skills are developed, they can simply be transferred to any other situation, whether it involves understanding the imperative in geography or the passive in history.

We need to know how far the skills of reading and writing, either in school or in the workplace, can stand as transferable and sustainable. Perhaps the very existence of ICT requires us to rethink where literacy belongs.

So who defines literacy (2)?

Ilana Snyder (1998) supports the latter position. She writes: '*Emerging literacies* takes as a starting point the understanding that the use of [new] technologies produces new literacies which we are only just beginning to identify and describe' (Snyder 1998: 25). Richard Hoggart expands this further: 'The simple conception of "literacy" so much promoted today is inadequate. At its best it is like a bag of fairly simple plumbers' tools, where we need a set of surgical instruments' (Hoggart 1998).

Catherine Beavis takes it a stage further. She is perfectly clear that print literacy is not simply 'not enough'. She argues that: '. . . multimedia and digital technologies are changing what we understand as literacy, so much so that our current understandings will be rendered obsolete' (Beavis

1998), a position echoed elsewhere in Lemke (1993, 1997); Luke (1996); Snyder (1996) and Lankshear and Knobel (2003).

We need to decide whether or not new technologies and new literacies are the order of the day or whether it is merely a question of context. Certainly, the KS3F places students in a print based context with rare venturings into the world of ICT based texts. Insofar as this is the definition of use, the KS3F, whatever your views of it as an education policy, addresses the needs it constructs as the experience of most students.

I referred earlier to the tensions in this document and want to draw your attention back to the declaration about 'life beyond school' . . . (KS3F: 9). In this context, it would be difficult to argue that ICT does not feature in most working, and indeed, leisure times of adults today. It is rare in the workplace, for example, that a text is produced by a single author, or that it relies solely on a linear model of reading and writing. It is more likely to be multi-authored, will often require an understanding of how to use presentation software such as PowerPoint, and will present itself as a text which has the possibility for hypertext links, a form of reading and writing which does not, therefore, have linearity as its model. If we are to accept that reading and writing in this context asks for a deeper understanding of the ways in which language works, we might heed the warnings of Margaret Meek:

> Now, instead of being encouraged to demonstrate the relation of reading and writing to new communication systems . . . teachers are overwhelmed by old-fashioned instructions, as cut and dried as anything proposed by the government inspectors in *Hard Times*.
>
> (Meek 1998: 116)

The case I wish to present acknowledges the position presented by the KS3F but challenges it too: if we are building a literate nation, how can we neglect ICT and its literacy demands?

As Papert in *The Children's Machine* states:

> What is true for individuals is even more true for nations. The competitive strength of a nation in the modern world is directly proportional to its learning capacity . . . the same technological revolution that has been responsible for the acute need for better learning also offers the means to take effective action.
>
> (Papert 1992)

Who monitors?

In part, of course, how literacy is defined in education is controlled by those responsible for monitoring the curriculum. The reality factor of the classroom often has to answer to imperatives which have little to do with professional judgement and everything to do with inspections, league tables and examinations. We also have to acknowledge that monitoring is not a straightforward notion. For example, in the UK, the range of Local Education Literacy Consultants are employed to 'support' teachers in developing 'effective' literacy skills through the use of government materials, pedagogical directives and methodological prescriptives. The line between 'support' and monitoring is fine. Indeed at an English conference in Australia (IFTE 2003), I heard an impressive presentation from a UK literacy consultant who felt her role to be bound by inflexible rules – all about delivering the government prescription, nothing about developing practice. She recounted how the teachers she was required to train were so angry with the training (not the trainer) they were required to attend that they sat with their backs to her as their only form of protest (Baranski 2003).

Similarly, teachers find themselves in a paradoxical position with the inspection of literacy. The KS3F has differing status in differing contexts. In initial teacher training, it is a *requirement* that trainees from all subjects be taught literacy in accordance with the KS3F. In schools, the KS3F is a *recommended* document only: schools are not required to implement it. Yet Ofsted (Office for Standards in Education) inspect schools for literacy provision and schools are expected, if they are not using the KS3F, to demonstrate how their literacy provision is equal to or better than that of the KS3F. The potential pitfalls are enormous. As an inspection sanity measure, most schools have chosen to implement the KS3F.

ICT figures either not at all or marginally in all of these monitored literacy demands. It is unsurprising that literacy therefore continues in many schools to be constructed as a print based, English department driven event. Unsurprising, but disappointing, is the missed potential to encourage all teachers to explore the potential of literacies in their subject and to do so by integrating the opportunities offered by ICT into that situation.

Who defines literacy (3)?

In an educational world increasingly controlled and defined by centralized policies, the type of literacy defined by the KS3F is undoubtedly one with which we in the UK at least have to deal. Margaret Meek refers to this type of literacy as 'schooled literacy' – the version of literacy required by and promoted through the curricula that exist in schools. ICT as *enhancing* 'schooled literacy' should not therefore be underestimated in potential significance in that it both allows us to address the policies and extend them into the wider ICT context. The model offered by the KS3F is one approach to literacy teaching. It enables teachers to meet the requirements of the policy documents but does not exploit what ICT could really do for literacy. In writing elsewhere about the relationship of ICT and literacy, I stated:

> ICT stands in interesting relation to literacy, being, as it is, capable both of supporting and promoting the basic skills of reading and writing – the dominant classroom definition of literacy (Papert 1993). Yet it carries with it the inevitability of extending that definition into a model of literacy which acknowledges, sine qua non, that literacy is a dynamic concept extending beyond the basic acquisition of reading and writing skills . . . that [this] is a limited interpretation of literacy and that the acquisition and development of literacy skills responds to a new taxonomy almost in direct response to the linking of ICT with literacy.
>
> (Brindley 2000: 11)

The 'new taxonomy' I offered drew on the notion that text within ICT is not static, nor linear, nor even containable (it is 'without margins'). It redefines text to include graphics, audio, hypertext, multiple authors, multiple representations of 'realities', text which confirms, extends and subverts itself. This version of text may be far removed from that of governments but it is not far removed from the experience of students. It may relate more to Papert's famous distinction between 'letteracy' ('the special skills involved in reading words made up of alphabetical letters') and 'literacy' ('. . . there are many literacies . . . writers have more recently suggested as substitutes . . . "ways of knowing"'). In this sense, the work that students do in schools called 'literacy' is misnamed – the acquisition of print based decoding skills sits a long way away from the skills which Papert contends constitutes real literacy – 'ways of knowing' (Papert 1992: 101).

Perhaps this is where you need to decide if, on your literacy spectrum, literacy is a set of skills or a concept flexible enough to recognize changing contexts. Is there a set of 'literacy skills' which can be applied to any situation, or are there specific skills needed to be a 'shrewd and fluent reader' or 'a confident writer' in the technological contexts of today? Perhaps the heart of this debate concerns literacy teaching simply to provide for a world economy – 'a life beyond school'. But in that 'life beyond school' it is unlikely any economic success stories will exist which do not require an understanding of literacy in relation to ICT.

Literacy and ICT: some implications

There is a growing understanding in literacy studies of the need to move beyond narrowly defined explanations of literacy to ones that capture the complexity of real literacy practices in contemporary society. Literacy needs to be conceived within a broader social order, what Brian Street and others have called a 'new communicative order'. In particular, this new communication order takes account of the literacy practices associated with screen-based technologies. It recognizes that reading and writing practices, conceived traditionally as print-based and logocentric, are only part of what people have to learn to be literate. For the first time in history, the written, oral and audiovisual modalities of communication are integrated into the same electronic system – multimodal hypertext systems made accessible via the internet and the World Wide Web. Being literate is to do with understanding how the different modalities are combined in complex ways to create meaning.

> If, we take '. . . account of the literacy practices associated with screen-based technologies', we need to consider which literacy skills we should be promoting.
>
> (Snyder 2001)

Beavis (2000) identifies five new types of literacies which, she claims, are required in a technology rich world: multimedia authoring skills, multimedia critical analysis, cyberspace exploration strategies and cyberspace navigation skills and the capacity to negotiate and deconstruct images, both visual and verbal.

Multimedia authoring skills require an understanding of how text and graphic interact: the ways in which they can be used together to support a message, or by positioning a text and graphic in opposition, subvert a message. This might be further enhanced by considering the need to teach multi-authoring in this context too. The common practice in the workplace of co-authoring is less often seen in schools compelled to assess on an individual basis. Nevertheless, this is the way that many texts are now constructed and is a literacy which currently is more often developed in the workplace than in schools. Possibly, such a situation may be one source of the complaint that students arrive from school without the literacy skills required in the twenty-first-century working environment.

Multimedia critical analysis calls not simply on ICT as a point of rethinking, but also on literacy. As Lankshear and Knobel in *Changing Literacies* state: '. . . literacies themselves vary enormously. Some of this variation is captured in broad qualitative categories and distinctions, such as "functional literacy" vs "cultural literacy" vs "critical literacy"' (Lankshear and Knobel 2003).

If we refer to the definition of critical literacy offered on the Tasmanian site for the Office for Curriculum, Leadership and Learning, which states that

> Critical literacy is an active, challenging approach to reading and textual practices. Critical literacy involves the analysis and critique of

the relationships among texts, language, power, social groups and social practices. It shows us ways of looking at written, visual, spoken, multimedia and performance texts to question and challenge the attitudes, values and beliefs that lie beneath the surface.

We can immediately see the inclusion of multimedia text as a 'given' in this government statement, itself an interesting development on the UK position. However, it also allows us to access one of the main purposes of literacy: to understand how language and image can be used to control. If literacy is to prepare us for effective language use, then it is essential to critically understand how language and image can be used to persuade, manipulate and, on occasions, indoctrinate.

This links directly with Beavis' next two categories, cyberspace exploration strategies and navigation skills. These are no mean skills to acquire. There cannot be many of us who haven't lost an hour or three to a fairly fruitless exploration of 'related' sites, emerging blinking as we realize that we have just wasted rather a lot of precious time reading incidental trivia, or just searching inefficiently. The skills of using search engines, identification of key words, logging sites used and so forth can be acquired by trial and error as many of us know, but efficient teaching of these strategies is important for an efficient use of the resource of the internet.

However, I should also like to suggest that cyberspace exploration is a highly sophisticated activity when it is also linked to building individual cognitive maps – literally linking sites together, perhaps in a mind map format, but which form intellectually dynamic sites – knowledge sites – which belong to the individual's personal intellectual quest. These thinking trails demonstrate microcognition, in the identification of the individual sites, but also metacognition, in the demonstration of links between those sites. Such higher order and creative thinking is a form of literacy rarely taught explicitly in schools – but the potential is enormous.

Beavis' final powerful literacy and ICT category, the capacity to negotiate and deconstruct images, both visual and verbal, takes us back to understanding: the capacity to recognize how and why collocations of text and image are being presented to us: to know how sites have been designed in order to understand why they have been designed in that way – what the intended impact on us is; to understand the rules of this new rhetoric so that we can resist or accept the messages we are given – but with good reason. In short, to read against the text so that we are able better to understand its intentions.

Many of these strategies will be familiar to English teachers whose working lives are bound up with understanding text, although the context and text representations, along with image, may not be so familiar. But to remind ourselves, literacy is for all teachers to promote. Without specific guidelines, we cannot automatically expect teachers not trained in textual analysis to be able to deal with these concepts. Nor can we expect this to happen without reference to the main reading material for many students these days – the internet. It seems, at the very least, a wasted opportunity for literacy if we do not consider how categories such as Beavis delineated can actually serve to enhance literacy learning and understanding beyond word, sentence and text level.

Conclusion

So where do we stand on the literacy spectrum? The linear line described by government policy holds that literacy is only marginally concerned with ICT. But perhaps we should re-define our terms at this point: ICT affords us not a simple range but a width and depth of understanding of the interaction of text with text, with image, with video, audio, animation – in fact, all forms of language that literacy asks us to engage with. So if you're standing on a uni-dimensional spectrum, perhaps now is the time to move into multi-dimensional literacy. It's surely where education belongs:

> If these technologies are sensitively and intelligently used, they have the potential to influence the whole development of the educational process – and with it, our collective futures.

> We will develop genuinely new skills ... These skills will rapidly approach the status of necessities, as without them it will become difficult to fully participate in society. Hence the genuinely literate person of this new century will have a facility with computers and visual images undreamed of in the last.
>
> (Puttnam 2001)

References

Beavis, C. (1998) Computer games, culture and curriculum, in I. Snyder (ed.) *Page to Screen*. London: Routledge.

Brindley, S. (2000) ICT and literacy, in N. Gamble and N. Easingwood (eds) *ICT and Literacy*. London: Continuum.

Davies, C. (1996) *What Is English Teaching?* Buckingham: Open University Press.

Department for Education and Employment (DfEE) (2001) *Framework for Teaching English, Years 7, 8 and 9*. London: DfEE Publications.

Gamble, N. and Easingwood, N. (2000) *ICT and Literacy*. London: Continuum.

Hoggart, R. (1998) Critical literacy and creative reading, in B. Cox (ed.) *Literacy Is Not Enough*. Manchester: Manchester University Press.

Lankshear, C., Gee, J., Knobel, M. and Searle, C. (1997) *Changing Literacies*. Buckingham: Open University Press.

Lankshear, C. and Knobel, M. (2003) *New Literacies: Changing Knowledge and Classroom Learning.* Buckingham: Open University Press.

Lemke, J. (1993) Critical social literacy for the new century, *English in Australia,* (105), September.

Lemke, J. (1997) Metamedia literacy: transforming meanings and media, in D. Reinking, L. Labbo, M. McKenna and R. Kiefer (eds) *Literacy for the 21st Century: Technological Transformation in a Post-typographic World.* Hillsdale, NJ: Erlbaum.

Luke, A. (1996) Text and discourse in education: an introduction to critical discourse analysis, in M. Apple (ed.) *Review of Research in Education 1995–6.* AERA.

Meek, M. (1998) Important reading lessons, in B. Cox (ed.) *Literacy Is Not Enough.* Manchester: Manchester University Press.

Papert, S. (1992) *Mindstorms.* London: Basic Books.

Papert, S. (1994) *The Children's Machine.* London: Basic Books.

Puttnam, D. (2001) Skills for life, *Literacy Today,* (23), June.

Snyder, I. (1996) *Hypertext: The Electronic Labyrinth.* Melbourne: Melbourne University Press.

Snyder, I. (1998) *Page to Screen: Taking Literacy into the Electronic Age.* London: Routledge.

Sunday Times Style Magazine (11 May 2003).

3

REDEFINING THE
'BASICS' OF ENGLISH

Geoff Barton

The changing nature of schooling

Welcome to the brave new world, in which schooling gives way to learning, and 'English teaching' becomes a quaint euphemism. Welcome to a changing educational world:

> What will be taught and learned; how it will be taught and learned; who will make use of schooling; and the position of the school in society – all of this will change greatly during the ensuing decades. Indeed, no other institution faces challenges as radical as those that will transform the school.
>
> (Drucker 1994)

Drucker's words fill you either with enormous optimism or anxiety. Whatever the emerging truth of his and other future thinkers' predictions, the only real certainty seems to be that there is no real certainty. Chaos rules.

So as change trembles beneath us, it challenges any long-held views of what English is and, more fundamentally, what it means to be either a student or a teacher. Just as the world our pupils inhabit is already different from the world we knew as children, so the adult world they will inherit will be one of unceasing and convulsive change. That surely is undeniable. On a personal level, my students can already gain much of the information they need from sources beyond me, most of it more reliable and more up-to-date than anything I can provide. And so in the process, my role as teacher is being reformulated, whether I like it or not, from the kind of role my own English teachers played in my education.

All the more reason then to be clear in our conception of what English is, and the essential skills and experiences we expect our students to gain from our work with them. This chapter explores current conceptions of English, the tensions as the ground shifts, and the liberating possibilities of ICT to help us to redefine the essential ingredients of the subject – the 'new basics'.

Computers and 'the basics'

Back in 1988 I got into a good-natured spat with Mike Peacock, then a researcher at the University of Leeds. He wrote an article in the *Times Educational Supplement* in which he cited a pupil's essay at GCSE grade F or G. Any attempt to grasp what the child was saying was seriously hampered by various technical weaknesses. The word processor, Mike Peacock argued, would eradicate such surface impediments to clarity and allow the reader to unlock the meaning within: ' "Is this cheating?" he asked. "Am I cheating because I drive to the seaside instead of walking?" ' (Peacock 1988).

This is a vision of information technology (we hadn't thought much about the 'communications' bit back then) as great liberator, helping pupils hampered by technical inaccuracy to produce work every bit as polished as everyone else's. Thus examination boards would no longer 'penalise the life-chances of those not born with enough of the necessary talent' (Peacock 1988). ICT would democratize achievement.

I replied in typically pompous fashion. You can't so readily separate form and content, I argued. Surface inaccuracy is linked to deeper issues; computers will never be able to identify grammatical errors (I got that one wrong); and the danger is that we stop teaching technical accuracy because of computers – what if these pupils don't later work with computers:

> they will be deprived of the spelling checker and the grammar watch-dog; their hand-written letters, spattered by spelling mistakes or gripped by ambiguities, will mark them out as members of a sub-class whose very distance from technology will highlight their lack of basic skills.
>
> (Barton 1988)

This was an early example of the way computers began to challenge our views of what English is and what we should be teaching young people. Mike Peacock saw computers reducing the emphasis on old-fashioned basic skills; I saw technical accuracy remaining as important as ever. The central part of the debate – what are the essential skills our pupils need in a changing world? – remain as relevant and unresolved as ever.

The answer depends, of course, on your view of what the world for which we are preparing students may be like, on your view of the function of schools, and on your conception of English.

Changing patterns of work and leisure

Charles Handy, speaking at the North of England Conference 2000, reminded us of future employment patterns, a world of what he describes as 'actors' careers. This will be a world of short-term, fixed contracts, picking up one job, completing it, moving to the next. The old careers are already dead: 'There are now more people in Britain in the creative industries earning £50 billion a year, more than the whole of British manufacturing industry. If you had said that twenty years ago no-one would have believed you' (Handy 2000).

Already, according to John West-Burnham, 60 per cent of new jobs are part-time; 40 per cent of all jobs are part-time. Thus the traditional path of school→[possibly university]→one firm→retirement is dead, just as the established route of student→teacher training→teacher-for-life looks increasingly fragile.

ICT already means that you do not have to go to an office to be an office worker. My office is, at intervals, a train, a hotel room, any available space anywhere where my laptop will fit. You no longer have to go to a bank to do your banking; and, of course, you do not have to go to university to be a university student.

As a result, nine to four schooling is becoming quaint, old-fangled, with learning needing to pervade our lives rather than be compartmentalized. The classroom need no longer be limited to the range of information available in a school room or library or resource centre. If there is a modem or certain phones, information can be obtained from anywhere in the world, 365 days a year – provided you have the skills and the access rights.

Global shifts mean that wealth already resides not in land or muscle power, but in knowledge. In the USA 20 per cent (those in analytical areas) earn 50 per cent of the total wealth of US citizens. The implication of this is a new social structure:

1. Top group – knowledge workers
2. Second tier – teachers, service industry managers

3. Third tier – manual workers
4. Fourth tier – unemployed.

This will be an era of new opportunities. But at the same time there looms the shadow of a new underclass, deprived of knowledge and the means to gain it. This in part explains the almost apocalyptic tone of much of the Department for Education and Skills' (DfES) justification for a more concerted approach to raising literacy levels. They talk of the weaknesses of the UK workforce in the basics; demonstrate the link between low literacy levels and crime and unemployment; and examine the economic consequences:

> In a report on the impact of literacy, education and training on the UK Economy, the accountants Ernst and Young estimate that 60 per cent of all jobs now require reasonable reading skills e.g. being able to understand and act on written instructions, obtain simple information and understand a price list . . . The report estimates the costs to the country of illiteracy, in lost business, remedial education, crime and benefit payments to be over £10 billion per annum
>
> (Ernst & Young 1993)

This is an argument driven not simply by economic expediency, as some critics would argue, but by fears of social breakdown – the social costs of **not** addressing basic literacy. This explains, I think, why the literacy strategy is driven with such fervour, and illuminates why the implementation is surrounded by such controversy.

A shift from English teachers to English learners

From the standpoint of English teachers, all of the preceding surely forces us to reflect upon our current practice. We need to decide what exactly we are teaching our current students, what they learn, what we are preparing them for and how effectively we do so. It is now absolutely clear that to be successful learners, our students will need to acquire specific skills and knowledge. We need to know how far these are different from those we taught in the past and whether or not the essentials of English are a set of unchanging certainties which can be applied in any context. There may be a need for us to update our methodology, to recast English in a new light.

All of these points might be synthesized perhaps in a single question: what do we mean by English? This question – an extraordinary one, I suspect, to most people outside education – has been a recurring theme of a century of English teaching. We need to know how far English should be about transmission of culture, should media form the new core and indeed how far content can be prescribed.

Until we have a clearer view of what we mean by English, we are unlikely to be certain of the skills our students need and our capacity to encourage them.

And more than in any other curriculum area, the question of what is English is inextricably linked with who teaches it. This isn't another of those 'what are English teachers like' articles; nor is it a critique of different models of English teaching. But in defining what we mean by English, we cannot ignore the question of who teaches it.

There is probably no more brooding cross-section of the teaching profession than English teachers. We brood, endlessly. Perhaps it's all that textual attention to dark works like *Hamlet* and *Wuthering Heights*; or the fact that so much of the English tradition in schools has been rooted in a humanistic approach, with heavy emphasis on personal response.

Perhaps our introspection derives from a wealth of literature not only about how we teach but also who we are. A number of key texts have, at different points, traced the development of English in schools: Margaret Mathieson's *Preachers of Culture* (1975), and, more recently, Bethan Marshall's *English Teachers: The Unofficial Guide* (2000).

Mathieson's title – a quotation from Matthew Arnold – says it all. English teachers have traditionally been charged with a social responsibility which stretches far beyond the mere transmission of skills and knowledge. *Preachers* hints at the evangelist, the impassioned communicator of a deeply-felt message. *Culture* is a deceptive and tantalizing word: every reader will see in it a world of her or his own making. For some it will signify imperialism, repression, the values of the state; others will infer high art – the great icons of human tradition; others will take 'culture' to mean the multi-media environment we inhabit. Whichever response we give to the word *culture*, there's something extraordinary in the underlying assumption about the English teacher's role. It imbues the English teacher with special responsibilities, and the language of a number of seminal writers on English teachers have caught some of this in their commentaries.

George Sampson, writing in 1921 in an England desperate for rebirth and regeneration, wrote: 'English is the one school subject in which we have to fight, not for a clear gain of knowledge, but for a precarious margin of advantage over powerful forces of evil.' English, he says, 'is not a subject at all. It is a condition of life.'

We remember F.R. Leavis's proclamations on the central place of English, particularly in higher education. More specifically, in the context of schools, David Holbrook was arguing for similar values, with creative writing helping pupils to tackle 'the backlog of psychic problems' (Holbrook 1967). This is English as psychotherapy-cum-spiritual renewal: 'The battle with the serpent,' he argued, 'is fought in the school' (Holbrook 1964).

Other commentators on English studies have continued to trace the development of English teachers' philosophical views. The well-known Open University Press series *English, Language and Education* provided a powerful sense through the 1980s and 1990s that to be an English teacher was to be charged with a special task. It had titles like *English at the Core*, *Thinking through English*, and *The Making of English Teachers*. The Cox Report, 1988, sorted English teachers into five broad philosophical groupings, and then shaped an initial national curriculum based on the dominant one, the 'personal growth model' (DES 1989).

Bethan Marshall's more recent investigation into the attitudes of English teachers shows a passion which is less dramatically expressed than Holbrook's but nonetheless charged with missionary zeal. Her approach employs an unusual method of categorizing the English teaching tradition and then using teachers' annotations on these philosophies in order to group respondents within certain headings. You get your Old Grammarians, Pragmatists, Technicians, Liberals, and Cultural Dissenters.

My point is not to explore any of these groupings, nor to give a critique of any of the philosophies. Instead it is to register the extraordinary nature of such a body of critical writing. There can be few if any other school subjects in which the focus of so much academic research is not the mode of teaching and learning, or the effectiveness of different strategies, but the nature of the teachers themselves. I wonder if teachers of, say, Personal and Social Education, or Geography, have a similar body of knowledge devoted to them. There is then a continuing tradition that English teachers are, in Margaret Mathieson's phrase, 'special people'. And this brings us to the heart of my contribution. What are the essential ingredients of English in the twenty-first century? What are the basics? And – a subsidiary but inescapable theme – who decides?

For if we are to explore the new basics of secondary English, we cannot avoid the associated issues of who teaches it and who controls it. And because of this rich tradition of a subject taught by 'special people', any suggestion that control is being wrested to the centre seems all the more provocative to many who see their vocation as embodying autonomy as well as responsibility.

Recent tensions in English

This is the centre of a debate concerning the introduction of the Government's National Literacy Strategy from Key Stages 1 and 2 into Key Stage 3, September 2001. The Framework for Teaching English Years 7 to 9 takes the broad objectives of the national curriculum for English and presents them in a method designed to encourage greater progression. This is a strategy not so much concerned with content, that is, after all, defined in the National Curriculum, but with teaching methodology.

What we encounter is, for many of us, a new style of teaching English, starting with ten-minute starter-lessons, rooted in word-level word exercises such as spelling lists. This then moves into a sequence of activities covering a range of reading, writing and speaking and listening skills, with a strong emphasis on rapid paced whole-class teaching.

People have reacted differently to the Framework. University lecturer Bethan Marshall led the assault in the *Times Educational Supplement* (27 April 2001) with dark warnings that English teachers would not accept lists of prescribed spellings across subject areas. The National Association of Teachers of English (NATE) was quoted in a main news page story on the BBC website (6 May 2001):

Anger over literacy 'hour'
The government faces protests from specialist English teachers over plans to introduce its literacy strategy into secondary schools from September.

The National Association for the Teaching of English (NATE) has warned ministers not to be 'over prescriptive' in its plans to change the way English is taught to 11- to 14-year-olds . . .

NATE says the new literacy strategy should not be allowed to take up more than 10 per cent of English lessons in secondary schools. Otherwise they fear the literacy element will swamp the wider subject of English.

This was not an entirely unexpected response, given the tradition of English teaching. As Jim Crowther and Lyn Tett have argued, literacy initiatives have tended to be perceived in three ways. First, they are represented as a cultural missionary activity (saving the illiterate from crime and unemployment); second as social control (creating more responsible, moral and productive citizens); and, third, literacy has been viewed as emancipation (freeing people from the state-controlled curricula). At the heart of this is the question of who defines English.

The critics of Government initiatives on literacy say that it marginalizes the expertise of the English teachers. It imposes a teaching framework which is rigid, mechanical and utilitarian. Its supporters would argue the opposite. They would claim that there is overwhelming evidence that traditional methodologies have failed significant numbers of students.

Greg Brooks' survey of literacy (1997) in the UK between 1948 and 1996 provides one useful summary. With literacy surveys dating from 1948 in the UK, there is an opportunity to take a wider perspective on literacy standards. Brooks concludes that literacy levels have changed little in that time, though there was some slippage among 8-year-olds (pupils in Year 3) in the late 1980s which was recovered in the early 1990s. The significant indicators of literacy levels are the international comparisons. These show a significant 'trailing edge' of underachievement. Whereas the UK is relatively successful in promoting middle- and high-performers, it is at the level of underachievers where literacy levels cause concern, international benchmarking suggests:

> The test was the same as that used in a survey of 27 other countries in 1991 (Elley, 1992) and includes narrative, expository (factual) and 'document' material (charts, tables, graphs, lists, etc.). This research has indicated that Britain is generally out-performed by countries like Finland, France and New Zealand. Britain is located within a 'middle' group of countries which includes Belgium and Spain. In the middle and upper parts of the range of scores, children in England and Wales performed as well as those in countries much higher in the rank order.
>
> (Brooks, Pugh and Schagen 1996: 13)

It is reasonable to ask if our investment in education is not preparing young people for the worlds of work and citizenship today, then how could it possibly deliver for the new challenges of the future?

Uncomfortable as this is for those of us who make our living from teaching English, there is a need to confront some unpalatable implications. First, in a changing world our definition of English needs to shift away from what English teachers want to teach. The focus needs to be on what skills and experiences our students need if they are to be successful participants in modern society.

Martin Tibbs, Chair of NATE, hinted at this in his address to the NATE conference, in April 2000. Based on his research into IT practice in France, the UK and Singapore, he interviewed employers about the skills they consider essential. Fascinatingly, there appeared to be a huge congruence between respondents in both Europe and Asia. All listed the following skills as being essential:

- literacy
- numeracy
- communication skills
- IT skills
- ability to work in a team
- self-knowledge and self-reliance
- ability to transfer skills into different contexts
- willingness to re-train ('Life Long Learning')

That was the Chair of NATE acknowledging some of the essential skills students need in the modern world. Surely part of our debate about English needs to address our role in providing those skills. This is what I define as a shift from the wishes of the teacher to needs of the learner.

In that context, there is something deeply child-centred, not utilitarian, about the new emphasis on literacy. Its focus is on the student, rather than the teacher. We need to know what the essentials of reading, writing, speaking and listening are that a child needs, irrespective of her or his teacher.

People who deny this are often attached to a sentimental and nostalgic view of English teaching. Like many of us in teaching they remember the teacher who inspired us, often our own English teacher. This is cause for celebration. It is why I became a teacher. But noble as the tradition of English teaching may be, it cannot be the main focus of curriculum planning and decision-making. In a world where students can circumvent us using ICT, the skills and experiences we *want* to teach are no longer the point.

The shift of emphasis from teaching to learning will therefore challenge much of our existing practice, hence the tensions we are seeing reported in the national media. The focus needs to be not on what I, the teacher, wish to teach; but rather on what my students need to learn. This in turn will lead us to reflect upon **how** they should best learn.

The new basics

For me, that is what the debate about English should now become: what are the essential skills and experiences our students need and how can they best learn them? In the process we should dispense with polarized thinking that views literacy as somehow separate from 'real' English and give a clear commitment that English has a responsibility to prepare students for the worlds of work and citizenship.

As a starting-point, the following would be my own nominations for the essential ingredients in a modern English curriculum.

1 Literacy

This is our first duty as English teachers. I think we can dismiss the narrow, utilitarian definitions of literacy. As Winston Brookes and Andy Goodwyn remind us: 'Its true definition encompasses much more than "basics" and may include "new" areas such as computer literacy, visual literacy, media literacy and so on' (Lankshear 1997).

The benefits of the National Literacy Strategy at Key Stages 1 and 2, now bedding in to Key Stage 3, are that it is rooted in research and that it has developed teachers' methodology. For the first time in several generations it becomes less easy to stand and unthinkingly replicate the teaching styles we ourselves experienced. Academics and the best teachers have always talked of the reflective practitioner: now, at last, we can reflect not only on content, but also on style, responding for ourselves to a methodology which challenges many of the assumptions of recent years (for example, that whole-class teaching is usually inappropriate). The basics of language will remain critical currency for our students. Exams may change, but will continue to exist. Employers will continue to need people who are analytical, good communicators, accurate, expressive and creative. The basics of English – the old-fashioned technical basics – are more important than ever. More than this, we need students who are adept at reading a range of texts, transforming them into different genres, identifying bias, reading critically; students who express themselves in speech and writing with clarity, creativity and precision; students who can use spoken language for confident and stylish effect, in a range of groupings. These skills are at the heart of our responsibility because they are the essential skills our students will need.

2 Heritage

This new world of uncertainties risks leaving all of us adrift. Our students need an embedded familiarity with the texts that have shaped our culture. They need to be able to make links between the present and the past. An emphasis on literacy is not to denigrate the cultural heritage, or to marginalize the best writers in our language. Instead, we must continue to view these authors as part of our students' entitlement, part of the new basics of English.

Adolescents remain, in John Adams' phrase 'incomplete' (1999). Part of our duty in helping them to orientate themselves in a fast-changing world is to provide anchor-points, texts which help them to define who they are, literature which provides a window on life.

Imaginative literature has always been at the heart of English teaching. We should reaffirm a commitment to it.

3 Metacognition

From anecdotal work in schools to influential works like Howard Gardner's *Frames of Mind: The Theory of Multiple Intelligences* (1984), we are realizing that traditional conceptions of intelligence do us few favours. Contemporary research into the workings of the brain, and studies of ways of empowering students to explore their own learning styles, should be embedded in the English curriculum. As John Adams put it, at the North of England Conference:

> We must focus on these new understandings about learning if we're to see in education reform massive opportunities, rather than still further problems. Within the last 10 to 15 years medical technology – positive emission tomography, CAT scans and functional MRI – has enabled us to *see* brains working. Instead of studying dead brains splayed out like

cold porridge on a dissecting table, we can actually see the incredible way in which, for instance, memory is distributed to many different regions of the brain, and how it is reconstructed on demand. Be you a creationist, or an evolutionist, the scale of this is awesome. What we can now *see* is more wondrous than anything we could earlier intimate from external observation.

(Adams 1999)

This is a huge and significant shift away from teaching towards learning.

English is the ideal forum for students to become more reflective about their growing abilities, more analytical in terms of their strengths and weaknesses, more self-conscious of teaching and learning styles that suit them. Hence my preoccupation with the need for English teachers to reflect more meaningfully on their own methodologies. Students need constantly to engage in discussion with us about how they are learning and how they can learn better. The language of learning – metacognition – should be central to the way we interact with students. In the process the teacher's role may change; but so should the student's – to a learner more centrally in control of her or his own development.

4 ICT

ICT is transforming our world. It is no longer enough for English simply to 'do word-processing'. Our students need to be thinking and communicating through ICT. As Julie Adams points out in her survey of ICT in Initial Teacher training: 'They [student teachers] thought that labelling some pictures from Clip-Art with nouns was a good use of IT' (Adams 1998).

Just as the Framework for Teaching English 11–14 places emphasis on students seeing teachers writing ('shared composition'), so our students need to see scaffolded ICT work. As Mary Simpson and Fran Payne put it: 'It appears that in the tutors' delivery of the courses, the students seldom experienced demonstrations of the use of ICT as a teaching tool – i.e. the tutors seldom modelled its use through their own practices' (Simpson et al. 1999).

The word-processing part of English is the easiest. But significant other opportunities remain. Some examples as to how students might use ICT:

- Online discussions of texts
- Building and analysing websites
- Making and then editing movies
- Exploring ICT genres – the language of email; computer jargon
- Active redrafting, editing and proof-reading
- Exploring different genres, using grammar and spelling programs to investigate the complexity or semantic fields of texts

- Exploring discourse structure actively by reshaping texts, moving sections or paragraphs around
- Investigating the way texts are made to cohere, identifying discourse markers using a computer
- Developing their own websites
- Investigating the language of emails
- Using software to interrogate sentence types
- Highlighting, changing, deleting connectives
- Re-ordering sentences within paragraphs
- Exploring tense
- Exploring modification, using phrases and clauses
- Exploring vocabulary using thesauruses, dictionaries, online reference sources
- Using software to catalogue texts, for example identifying the overall reading level of a document

Most important is the principle that ICT is as central to the English curriculum as to any other subject area, both as a tool for learning, and as a source of texts for exploration. The days of it helping us to perform secretarial skills are over: it is now in itself a mode of learning, a part of our teaching methodology.

Conclusion

In the schools of the present, many of the old arguments about teacher autonomy are discredited and unjustifiable. A changing world needs a different view of English – one more rooted in the needs of the learner than the wishes of the teacher. As Michael Fullan has noted, for too many teachers in our schools, 25 years of experience has actually meant one year's experience duplicated 25 times. This kind of stasis is no more acceptable than visiting a doctor who insists on using the same research, the same medical practice, or the same equipment as she used when she trained. The English teacher of the present needs to be extraordinarily accomplished and up-to-date with research about learning, pedagogy, and ICT.

None of this is to deny the central importance of the English teacher, still for me one of the most significant and influential roles in school, but it does suggest that it is time to redraw the battle-lines, and rethink our responsibilities in terms of our students' needs.

Theirs, after all, will be an age of uncertainty and unceasing change. Hence the need for secure literacy and communication skills. Hence the need also for deep links to their heritage, an anchor-point in an unstable world. Learning is bursting out from the artificial confines of the school day. New technology will liberate ongoing learning at work and at home, around the clock. Part of our task, therefore, is to teach our students about learning, that is, metacognition. And finally we have a fourth responsibility: ICT. It is no longer adequate for English teachers to claim that word-processing is their only possible contribution. ICT enables students actively and interactively to explore and deconstruct texts; then to create their own. These processes have always been central to English: now we need to embrace the new technologies to achieve them faster and better.

All of which reaffirms the responsibilities of the English teacher, and poses a significant challenge in terms of training and recruitment. But those are bigger issues. The main concern for now is to harness the talents of a committed and energetic body of English teachers, and focus their energies on the specific needs of young people today. There can be no greater mission.

References

Adams, J. (1998) ICT in initial teacher training – the new standards for the award of Qualified Teacher Status (QTS). Paper presented to British Educational Research Association (BERA) Conference, Belfast.

Adams, J. (1999) Battery hens or free range chickens: what type of education for what type of work? Keynote speech at North of England Education Conference, Sunderland.

Baker, M. (2001) BBC News website: www.news.bbc.co.uk, 6 May.

Barton, G. (1988) Beware the word-processor. *Times Educational Supplement*, 24 June.

Brookes, W. and Goodwyn, A. (1998) Literacy in the secondary school. Paper presented to British Educational Research Association (BERA) Conference, Belfast.

Brooks, G. (1997) Trends in standards of literacy in the United Kingdom, 1948–1996. National Foundation for Educational Research. Paper presented to UK Reading Association Conference, Manchester.

Cox, M. (1999) in M. Leask and N. Pachler (eds) *Learning to Teach Using ICT in the Secondary School*. London: Routledge.

Crowther, J. and Tett, L. (2000) Developing critical literacy in the context of Democratic Renewal in Scotland. Paper in 28th Annual SCUTREA Conference.

Department for Education and Employment (DfEE) (1999) *National Literacy Strategy: Review of Research and Other Related Evidence*. www.standards.dfee.gov.uk

Department of Education and Science (DES) (1989) *English for Ages 5–16* (The Cox Report). London: HMSO.

Drucker, P. (1994) *Post Capitalist Society*. London: Harper.

Gardner, H. (1984) *Frames of Mind: The Theory of Multiple Intelligences*. London: Heinemann.

Handy, C. (2000) The world around the corner: how best to prepare for it? North of England Conference.

Holbrook, D. (1967) *Creative Writing*. London: Cambridge University Press.

Holbrook, D. (1964) *Secret Places*. London: Methuen.

Marshall, B. (2000) *English Teacher – The Unofficial Guide: Researching the Philosophies of English Teachers*. London: RoutledgeFalmer.

Marshall, B. (2001) *Times Educational Supplement*, 27 April.

Mathieson, M. (1975) *The Preachers of Culture*. London: Unwin Allen.

Peacock, M. (1988) *Times Educational Supplement – English Extra*, 20 May.

Sampson, G. (1921) *English for the English*. Cambridge: Cambridge University Press.

Simpson, M., Payne, F., Munro, R. and Hughes, S. (1999) Using information and communications technology as a pedagogical tool – who educates the educators? Paper presented to European Conference on Educational Research, Finland.

Tibbs, M. (2000) Off-beam or on target? Summary of Chair's speech to National Association for Teaching English (NATE) Annual Conference, April.

West-Burnham, J., *The Changing Nature of Schools*, unpublished paper, University of Hull.

4

SECONDARY SCHOOL CASE STUDIES OF LITERACY AND ICT

Alison Tyldesley and Chris Turner

Introduction

Literacy is currently at the forefront of the British government's plans to improve secondary education. The National Literacy Strategy (DfEE 2001) has been extended to secondary schools in a move to improve national standards as measured by national tests. ICT is a key aspect of the drive to improve standards through increased funding to schools and additional staff training. This chapter provides case studies of good practice in using ICT in literacy teaching and learning in secondary schools (11–16-year-olds). The case studies illustrate situations where ICT has contributed to three key principles of teaching and learning described by the Teacher Training Agency (1998), namely:

1. supporting good practice in subject teaching;
2. a direct relationship between the use of ICT and teaching and learning objectives;
3. using ICT so that teacher or pupil can achieve something that could not be achieved without its use.

Material for the case studies was obtained through interviews with teachers and pupils, classroom observation and examination of documents and materials provided by the schools. The names of schools are fictional.

The experience has provided fresh insights and understandings about the exciting role that ICT can play in teaching and learning in literacy.

Case Study 1: Tennyson School, literacy learning and interactive whiteboards

Tennyson School in Sheffield is an example of a mixed catchment secondary school engaging with the process of implementing a range of initiatives promoted by the Literacy Strategy. One initiative includes implementing *Literacy Progress Units* (DfES 2001). These units were designed for pupils entering secondary school below Level 4 of the National Curriculum (DfEE 1999). In other words, they are 'catch-up' materials designed to support pupils who have fallen behind with Literacy skills. The units are designed to be taught in twenty minute slots to small groups of pupils three times per week. This presents organizational difficulties in terms of finding appropriate times when pupils will not miss out on other curriculum entitlements.

At Tennyson School the first stage in implementing the programme was to identify pupils who would benefit from the programme. Groups of six pupils were identified from the same classes and the programme carried out in registration periods. Literacy Progress Units are an example of heavily prescribed teaching materials designed by the National Literacy Strategy. They provide 'teaching scripts' and are linked to very specific teaching objectives from the National Literacy Strategy Primary Framework (DfEE 1998). The assumption is made that all pupils achieving level 3 at the end of Primary school need to catch up with the same objectives. The experienced staff at Tennyson School who are implementing these units consider they contain extremely good material. Their main criticism of the units is that the designated twenty minute time slots do not give them enough time to build on previous learning and consolidate learning before moving on to the next teaching point. The Office for Standards in Education evaluated the first year of the pilot Key Stage 3 Strategy (OFSTED 2002) and made similar comments. OFSTED noted there was often too much to be covered for the length of session proposed.

Tennyson School not only decided to surmount the practical difficulties involved in implementing these units, but also determined to take advantage of new facilities provided in a City Learning Centre. These facilities included purpose built classrooms with interactive whiteboards. Teachers delivering Literacy Progress Units were given technical support to download all the unit material onto computers so that the interactive whiteboard could be used rather than overhead projector slides.

Using interactive whiteboards created several advantages over traditional methods. The units were designed to be copied onto overhead projector slides. With an interactive whiteboard, texts can appear directly on screen or whiteboard. The primary advantages were the clarity and visibility of the image, and the speed and effectiveness with which snippets of text could be highlighted and deleted. The use of colour gives an added dimension and in the case of units of work on spelling colour was used to highlight suffixes, prefixes or examples of pluralization.

The teachers were still learning the range of techniques that draw attention to features of the text. The results were extremely effective. For example, they started to use a tool which acts like a window blind that moves up or down and gradually reveals text. This focused pupils' attention more intently on the whiteboard and encouraged them to look more carefully at the visual or morphemic nature of spelling patterns. The whiteboard pens enabled teachers and pupils to hand-write on the board and save material until the next lesson for review and dis-cussion. All these factors gave teachers flexibility over pre-determined materials.

The Key Stage 3 manager at Tennyson School described the use of ICT thus: 'It gives a modern feeling to what we are doing. We can save work and remind pupils of what they did in the last lesson.' The teachers identified the practical benefits arising from using ICT with pre-prepared teaching materials. All unit lessons were saved on hard disc and so were instantly available. Access to materials was more straightforward. The primary advantage, however, for both teaching and learning was seen to be the visual impact of materials.

The interactive whiteboard was seen to affect teaching styles. Modelling to explain the rules and conventions of language and texts was easier and reading and writing techniques could be demonstrated effectively. Teachers felt they could enhance their existing teaching styles and believed they were building on best teaching practice. The units on improving writing and comprehension of reading included activities which enabled text annotation and editing and made modelling these processes more transparent and explicit.

Ongoing learning assessment was also supported by ICT as reviewing learning became more explicit. During any lesson, screens could be reloaded which summarized key points from the previous session. Pupils' misconceptions could be easily picked up as they responded to 'deliberate' errors made by the teacher or wrote on the interactive whiteboard themselves.

The pupils had strong views on the benefits of the technologies they were using. They commented on the advantages of the interactive whiteboard compared to overhead projectors used in a previous Literacy Progress Unit. We include some comments from pupils who were interviewed:

If you just use an overhead projector it's kind of boring and that's [whiteboard] kind of exciting and you look at it more. It's fast and it helps me remember things.

It's got all exciting things. If someone nudges an overhead projector it moves out of the way but this helps you because you can see it and because it's got nice colours.

The teachers noted improved motivation and fascination created by technology use particularly in the case of the boys involved in the programme. The KS3 manager noted that boys often knew more than she did about what to press and offered helpful comments such as, 'You just need to click on this, Miss.'

Assessment had not at that time been carried out on the impact of the Literacy Progress Units on pupils' attainment. The effect of using ICT in combination with teaching specifically targeted literacy lessons cannot be formally evaluated as there are no control groups in operation. However, teachers reported their perception of the benefits to learning. They saw the prime benefit being improved motivation, interest and engagement and noted that from experience increased engagement leads to improved attainment.

Summary comments from the KS3 manager included the fact that using ICT had increased the status of the Literacy Progress Unit work and given it a more professional touch. She indicated pupils' positive attitudes to the programme. She had seen no evidence of reluctance to attend sessions, whereas her previous experience was that pupils disliked being singled out and given special treatment. She commented:

I don't think the other kids have the impression that this is something inferior because the pupils who are getting extra support are taught in 'special' rooms in the City Learning Centre.

OFSTED completed some national evaluation of the Literacy Progress Units and commented on clear evidence of their positive impact on confidence and self esteem (2002). The impact of delivering the units using ICT had no formal evaluation. However, there was a great deal of enthusiasm from both teachers and pupils at Tennyson School and the reported perception was that the novelty was not wearing off.

Case Study 2: Wordsworth High School, ICT and comprehension

Wordsworth High School, an 11–16 comprehensive school, is situated in a leafy suburb in the south of Greater Manchester. The school achieves high examination results and the English Department has benefited from excellent and innovative leadership over recent years. The Department has a policy of using ICT in English, with ideas for lessons and stimulating articles to read. The Department is well on its way to having an ICT component in every Unit of Study. It is, therefore, just the kind of school and English Department where one would expect interesting and exciting things to be happening with ICT.

A mixed ability Year 8 class of 11 boys and 12 girls, all aged 12 or 13, were in the ICT facility for their last lesson of the day, to continue their study of argumentative styles of writing. They were exploring the history of boxing, drawing out the arguments for and against its continuation as a legal sport in the UK.

The experienced teacher was also at ease with ICT. She defined the learning aims for the lesson as:

• to know how to use Encarta [a digital encyclopedia, published by Microsoft];
• to understand the history and rules of boxing as a background to a written assignment;
• to be able to record relevant details for future use in the assignment.

In this lesson ICT provided the necessary reading material. The teacher's task sheet also highlighted the fact that pupils would need to know how to access the necessary texts from the copy of Encarta on the school's intranet.

Pupils were guided to consider the relevant information by a series of questions on the lesson task sheet. The sheet also contained details of a final activity in which pupils were to use special word processing features to tabulate the outcomes of their consideration of the issues for and against boxing. Finally, if all that were successfully completed, pupils could access the internet in search of additional and relevant material on boxing for the assignment.

The main activity looked very much like a typical, old-style comprehension activity: pupils read and answered questions on a passage, and were required to write answers in their own words. It would be easy to be critical, and question the role of ICT in this process. Is it doing anything significant, or is this lesson simply reductive and decontextualized comprehension by any other name? Closer examination revealed fascinating insights into reading processes and the contribution ICT can make to the development of reading skills.

First, the text the pupils were reading was not a 'typical' comprehension passage. It was not decontextualized; the pupils knew both why they were reading it and also its relevance to a sequence of lessons leading to a known objective, a piece of writing on the arguments for and against boxing.

Second, the Encarta text made use of its digital format to include pictures, as well as 'clickable links' to other information. Pupils, therefore, had to choose how much and to what depth to read and explore.

Third, the limitations of the 'screenful' of text meant that pupils had to learn to cope by scrolling up and down the text in their search for information. It may seem an obvious requirement to anyone familiar with reading computer screens, but it is an important additional reading skill for coping with digital texts, a skill acquired and practised in just such an activity as described earlier.

When asked, pupils could articulate some interesting ideas on the advantages of using ICT for this task. Some thought it was easier to find information on the screen and at the computer, while others thought they were given scope to find information for themselves from the available resources.

Observations revealed that pupils scrolled up and down the text as they skimmed and scanned, clicked on links to see what was there, and re-read earlier parts of the document in search of answers. In fact, they were using a range of reading strategies very effectively, including the deployment of distinctive reading skills for this context.

Case Study 3: Coleridge School, oracy and PowerPoint

Coleridge School is a secondary school in Sheffield benefiting from increased funding to develop ICT use. The literacy coordinator described the catchment area as 'disadvantaged' with a large number of pupils on the special needs register. The school has had an intensive focus on all aspects of literacy and has extended their work into upper school groups, developing new initiatives to enhance pupils' writing, reading and oral presentation skills. The pupils involved in this project were 15-year-olds. The focus of the work was persuasive texts and preparing a presentation for an audience. The students worked in pairs and used multimedia software.

The literacy coordinator justified the emphasis on oral work by commenting on the pupils' strong regional accent and use of colloquialisms and non Standard English. He noted: 'Whilst the local accent adds vigour and structure to debate and dialogue, when it impinges on writing style it can damage a student's potential for academic success.'

This project was carried out as a unit of work over several English lessons. A role-play situation was set up in which students were asked to consider the possibility of starting their own company. The end product of the unit of work was to be a professional business presentation given to a group of potential investors with the aim of persuading them to invest in the company. The importance of a realistic context was stressed and the necessity for a high quality presentation. Ideas were developed about using language to convince, persuade and manipulate an audience. The teacher chose to use Microsoft PowerPoint, a presentation program which allows the user to mix text, graphics, sound and moving images. Slides can be projected on to a screen from a computer as part of a lecture or presentation.

The students needed to learn how to organize and use a PowerPoint presentation. They were allowed time to work on their presentations. A lesson was provided on oral presentation skills focusing on body language and position, voice projection, use of formal Standard English and practical management of the computer and screen. The literacy coordinator listed the advantages of using ICT to promote oracy and literacy. He noted that use of ICT enhanced specific learning objectives and scaffolded the oral task, adding realism, work-related relevance and the possibility of achieving a professional end product.

The presentations themselves achieved a high level of professionalism incorporating persuasive devices such as alliterative jingles, well-organized subheadings, rhetorical questions and eye-catching images. The students chose a wide range of businesses as the basis of their presentations including mobile phone companies, clothes shops, travel agents, take-away food and night-clubs. They could draw on their knowledge of advertising in choice of layout and language features. An example of their appropriate use of persuasive language includes this quotation from a PowerPoint slide:

About Your Phone Selection
• Stylish yet practical
• Suave and sophisticated
• Sexy yet open-minded
• Customisable
• No 2 phones the same

The students responded very positively to the sense of purpose and practical nature of the assignment. They were motivated to search for appropriate visual images and researched the use of techniques involved in successful marketing. They could analyse how the use of ICT had helped develop their presentational skills.

Students responded to questions about the effectiveness of using ICT by noting that it was more fun and motivating. One said it supported 'visual learning' and gave a sharp and bright image. The same student compared the use of PowerPoint with a similar purely oral presentation: 'I did this a few years ago but it were hand-written and that and people were talking amongst themselves and it were quite boring. With this we got a proper speech written out and we had more time because we were doing it on a computer [sic].'

Students noted that it looked 'more flashy' and that people were much more likely to pay attention and take you seriously if you were presenting on PowerPoint rather than holding up a series of pictures. They claimed it improved presentation skills and therefore confidence and supported organization, 'so that "you didn't need to 'faff' around with papers."' They also commented on the process of creating slides and planning. Comments were made about the editing power and potential and the benefits of searching the internet for information.

The real context of the task was seen as leading to increased motivation:

> We are getting better at persuasive language because we're trying to persuade someone to buy our business. We learnt how to use positive, persuasive language. We described the business with positive words. You had to try and write it like you're doing something for them.

The pupils' own responses were a testimony to principles of good ICT use. They commented that ICT had supported their learning and was related to clear objectives about using persuasive language. They were also very clear that the use of ICT enabled them to achieve something that would have been much less effective as an oral presentation supported with overhead projector slides. This case study is an example both of a well thought out use of ICT to support Literacy and Speaking and Listening objectives and also of good practice that appears to impact on more effective learning and motivation.

Case Study 4: PowerPoint across the sea

This case study concerns a trainee teacher in 2000–2001. Towards the end of her 36-week course she was required to develop some innovative teaching and learning opportunities in conjunction with English teachers in a secondary school. She was interested in developing approaches to using ICT in English, in particular producing materials that could be used with her secondary students in a Mexican school where she was to begin her career.

She undertook her second school experience in an 11–16 comprehensive school in a residential area of North Manchester. The school had a tradition of examination success, and a strong ethos of commitment to excellence in discipline and achievement. The Year 9 students she worked with were some of the most able in the year.

Microsoft's presentation program, PowerPoint was used in this project also. Some Year 9 students were asked to create PowerPoint presentations that exemplified their life in a major English city, knowing that their presentations would be viewed by students in a very different country.

The trainee teacher was very clear about what she wanted to achieve in her innovative project: to explore the effectiveness of PowerPoint for this particular purpose. Two main challenges emerged:

1. how best to make students aware of the features and potential of PowerPoint;
2. how students could discover the kinds of texts they might create with the software.

She planned to record the presentations on CD-ROM, for ease of transportation to Mexico and then to use the Manchester work as examples to be explored and replicated by the Mexican students, with Mexican presentations to be sent back to the Manchester school. The plans were achieved and this section draws on:

- the teaching plans used, notes, and examples;
- the Manchester PowerPoint presentations;
- the Mexican PowerPoint presentations;
- material written while the Mexican students were in process of preparing their presentations.

What emerges strongly from these materials is a sense of exploration and discovery of the possibilities of the software, and of new kinds of texts that could be created. Both aspects are inextricably interlocked, and the outcomes of the blend most exciting.

The teaching notes stated that a major objective was '. . . that students should use ICT as a medium to connect with young people living across the globe – students to be aware of the implications of that with regard to ICT.' So she set herself the task of creating an example presentation to show her students. She deliberately incorporated as many features of the program as possible, to reveal its possibilities as well as familiarizing herself with its features and how to use them. She acknowledged that the students would undoubtedly know about or would discover additional features of the program, so she planned for moments to share discoveries with the whole group.

After exploring her sample presentation with her students, she gave them time to tackle the task specifics, namely, 'To create a series of slides (using PowerPoint) about our daily lives and where we live for pupils in Mexico City.' The students had five 60-minute lessons plus homework time to complete the task. They could work individually or in pairs/small groups, with access to a computer suite for all five lessons.

Clearly the Manchester students had no problems working with words, sounds, and pictures, though there was some need to 'fine tune' the presentations. Students enjoyed choosing animation and transition effects, as well as selecting sounds and images. There is also evidence of an awareness of design features, especially in the positioning of items on the slide. What comes across is a sense of the students' zestful creativity in experimenting with the possibilities.

All the Manchester students created sequential texts, that is, following the format of a book, so that one slide followed on from another.

PowerPoint is designed to be used in that way, of course, as it is expected that the slides will be presented to an audience one after the other, with the presenter in charge of the changeover from one slide to the next. A similar sequence of teaching and learning activities was followed with the Mexican students. Quite evidently they used the Manchester templates very effectively for their own purposes. However, one student offered a very different kind of text, making use of the PowerPoint facility to create hyperlinks. He created an opening slide that acted as a home page from which the reader could make choices as to which piece of information to read next. His slide show stood out not only because he had done something different from the majority, but also because he made use of his awareness that PowerPoint presentations can be read as well as viewed, on one's own as well as part of an audience.

There is no doubting the motivational effect of creating texts for a defined audience or readership. There is then a clear purpose for using the software to complete the task, and the very real possibility of feedback and responses.

Teachers, in addition, have a responsibility in the National Curriculum for English to introduce students to as broad a range of texts as possible. The National Literacy Strategy advocates a pedagogy that provides classes with exemplars of new texts that can be explored and examined with the teacher, with further exploration independently or in small groups. Finally, students need to apply their discoveries about texts in their own creations, thus showing understanding of textual features and linguistic choices for defined purposes and audiences/readerships.

Everything that occurred in Manchester and Mexico with the technology exemplifies those long held principles of good English/Literacy teaching, namely that students apply themselves best when they have a sense of audience (at best, a real audience), purpose, and context for study and especially for writing.

Case Study 5: Using computer-generated simulations

This case study draws on a range of experiences using computer generated simulations (CGSs) with school students, trainee secondary English teachers, and experienced teachers as part of an in-service programme. Unlike the other case studies, this section is not based on specifically observed lessons. Rather, it uses a range of experiences to reveal essential features of CGSs, and their advantages that apply whoever is taking part. Finally, we consider what elements of ICT contribute to the literacy learning that can be stimulated by CGSs.

To run a simulation, it is enough to have one computer and printer in the classroom with a full class of participants. Controlled by the program, the computer periodically comes to life, making noises, and printing out messages, imitating the kind of teleprinter newsfeed that used to be found in many newsrooms.

Participants work in groups to solve a problem. In one simulation, students have to prepare a radio news bulletin from the stream of information items provided by the computer. Another example requires participants to behave like a team of police officers as they try to solve a murder from evidence (for example: sightings, forensic reports, witness statements) provided periodically by the computer. Another simlation gets students investigating why a group of children left home for school but did not arrive, requiring map reading skills as well as considerations of safety issues and behaviour. A further development of this type of program enables a class to participate in an inquest based on a Shakespeare play. There are yet other varieties of the genre. The following claims are made for this computer use:

- The computer drives the lesson by providing the resources for the task;
- There is something special about the 'hook' of the computer bleeping into life and a printer churning out yet more information or a contradictory view;
- Students have to focus as there is so much information coming their way;
- Good group work skills are essential;
- The teacher is able to use the opportunity to observe the class, systematically monitor pupils, or do some assessments of, for example, oral skills;
- A wide range of reading, writing, and oracy skills have to be used throughout the duration of the simulation;
- If roles are developed, a range of drama skills can be brought into play.

Secondary school students must be prepared very carefully for what is to happen. Teachers need to consider group roles and writing demands, especially if reports have to be written and students have little idea about what constitutes a report.

The actual experience of the CGS is usually hectic. One member of each group brings the latest snippet of information to the group and ensures that each person knows the update. The group has to manage 'information overload' as print-outs stream from the printer. At times there can be an unbroken sequence of messages, followed by long pauses when nothing emerges from the computer.

Participants, however, are quickly involved, and it is interesting to note the language and discourse features employed to cope with the CGS demands. The way groups manage the challenge of the task can be enlightening, especially when participants employ imaginative solutions to piles of paper, or future managers hone their emerging skills in face of deadline pressures.

The requirement to re-read in the light of new information is a skill that can be difficult to practise in other circumstances and is one of the most effective examples of reading skills needed in such simulations.

Students rely particularly on writing activities to help them manage the data stream, for example lists are made, time-lines created, and items cross-referenced. There is usually a specific writing demand that accompanies the simulation, for example, a radio news bulletin that needs a script (that keeps changing as new information emerges just before the deadline!), or interim report writing prompted by a pause from the computer.

A wide range of oral skills have context and purpose in a CGS, with opportunities to develop a range of distinctive skills. At times, particular questions predominate; in the early stages, there are many orienting and information gathering questions ('Where is the living room on the plan?' 'What's the name of Juliet's mother?'), while later on pupils begin to hypothesize about likely events and scenarios ('If Ralph is the murderer, how do you explain where he left his car that night?').

There are times when it seems to get too much for some people – too much information which won't make sense, and a deadline fast approaching. Language is then often used to support the group dynamic at a moment of crisis, and some students reveal subtle linguistic nuances as they cajole, challenge, uplift, and help each other.

Finally, there are the specific language demands of the final product, including two minute radio news bulletins, prepared speeches to an inquiry, questions for a hot seated character, presentations, and reflections on the whole process. Writing tasks are generally enlivened by the experience, and teachers can be as imaginative as ever when thinking about appropriate follow up writing in a variety of styles for a range of purposes.

In a sense, ICT has contributed at a very basic level, that is, using a program to print out pieces of text at preset timed intervals. The programs themselves are very simple and often there is minimal contact with the computer. It can be argued that this rather crude use of ICT actually stimulates a wider range of aspects of literacy learning, and that it exemplifies how technology can promote learning without getting in the way, without becoming too much the centre of attention. It is salutary to be reminded that we need to keep the focus on students' experiences and learning, rather than be dazzled by the glare of technological wizardry. What is needed is harmony, so that both teaching and learning are enhanced by the use of ICT in imaginative and principled ways.

Conclusions

We cannot ignore the range of different kinds of texts that we all, children and adults, encounter daily. Some digital texts, such as hypertext, multimedia texts and web pages, have very distinctive features, and we need to exploit their possibilities to our students' advantage. Digital texts are easy to send via email and lend themselves to being easily published on the internet, with consequential ease of access. Such texts make use of some distinctive styles of 'writing' or creating, involving manipulation that goes way beyond the straightforward use of pen or word processor. A whole set of visual and design imperatives comes into play, requiring experience of similar products for evaluation purposes and for examples of good practice. In other words, we can argue that a range of skills and aptitudes is brought into play when such texts are created, skills that may reside in an individual or a collaborative group.

Such skills must be seen as closely allied with writing, understood in its traditional sense of pen or pencil marks on paper. We are, in effect, broadening the definition of 'writing', thus adding to our students' repertoire of styles to choose from as appropriate.

With those thoughts in mind, these lessons demonstrate at least two very important facets of using ICT in literacy:

1. ICT must contribute something distinctive to learning in literacy for it to be pedagogically effective and justifiable.
2. Sometimes we have to look very hard to see the special contribution.

The case study lessons, taken at random in the sense that the writers were dependent on teachers allowing them to visit their classes, do demonstrate that ICT can enhance and significantly develop learning in the domain of literacy. They are not meant to be models, although it is claimed that significant applications of ICT are in operation, with identifiable effects in terms of students' learning and positive attitudes. Although the studies spring from very different contexts and a range of purposes for using ICT in Literacy, nevertheless there are some features of these lessons that are worth identifying as distinctive and pedagogically special.

It is worth noting how aware students were that they were being asked to approach tasks in different ways. We should always be constantly amazed at the ability and readiness of students to reflect on their own learning, and see the advantages of the chosen strategy or task. In one case study, it was only when students' responses were analysed that the distinctiveness emerged.

Second, it pays to search carefully when looking to define the difference that ICT can make to learning and teaching in secondary English. Students' perceptions of the contribution of ICT can be most illuminating, and can give a fresh impetus to reflections on pedagogic rationales for the ICT choices we make. However, we need to keep the focus on aspects of students' progress in literacy, and then seek out how ICT contributes its distinctiveness.

Finally, use of ICT can aid communication and help break down stereotypical thinking. The Mexican students in preparing to create their own PowerPoint presentations evaluated the offerings of their Manchester peers. To help them frame their thinking and their responses, their teacher helpfully provided a response sheet set out in tabular form with key prompt questions and spaces for answers. These notes were then used for subsequent writing. One student was very forthright in using this opportunity to set the record straight:

> Since I assume they have never come [sic] I think it would be rather interesting to tell them how is Mexico, Mexico City and its attractions. I would explain to them we do not live in clay or straw houses, that we do not go around on donkeys, that we don't wear a sombrero, that we have technology and that we do not have dirt roads.

If this project, and its use of ICT to exchange digital texts across the world, helps in some small way to break down stereotypes and bring students from two countries closer together, then digital technology will have done us all a great service, and used its special features to good effect in that cause.

References

Department for Education and Employment (DfEE) (1998) *National Literacy Strategy: Framework for Teaching*. London: DfEE Publications.

Department for Education and Employment (DfEE) (1999) *The National Curriculum: English*. London: DfEE and QCA Publications.

Department for Education and Employment (DfEE) (2001a) *Key Stage 3 National Strategy; Framework for Teaching English: Years 7, 8 and 9*. London: DfEE Publications.

Department for Education and Employment (DfEE) (2001b) *Key Stage 3 National Strategy: Literacy Progress Units*. London: DfEE Publications.

Office for Standards in Education (OFSTED) (2002) *The Key Stage 3 Strategy: Evaluation of the First Year of the Pilot*. London: OFSTED Publications (available at www.ofsted.gov.uk).

Teacher Training Agency (TTA) (1998) *Using Information and Communications Technology to Meet Teaching Objectives in English Initial Teacher Training: Secondary*. London: TTA Publications.

5

USING COMPUTERS TO ASSIST IN DEVELOPING KEY LITERACY SKILLS

Aisha Walker and Rachel Pilkington

Introduction

Literacy may be defined as the set of skills needed to process information effectively using the communications media and language(s) of the given culture. In this highly technological age, being fully literate includes being confident in computer use and Computer Mediated Communication (CMC) (Warschauer 1999). However, there are many young people in Britain (and elsewhere) whose educational potential is stifled by a 'literacy deficit', in which reading comprehension and written communication skills may lag behind other skills development. These pupils may articulate their opinions in spoken debate yet lack the tools to express themselves clearly in writing. This chapter addresses the question of whether text-based computer mediated communication (CMC) can enhance literacy skills by motivating students to extend their oral debating skills in ways that scaffold the development of written argument. We present and discuss work at an out-of-school learning support project to develop key literacy skills amongst secondary school children.

Other researchers have suggested important benefits may be associated with the use of CMC through encouraging inclusive participation in debate and the creation of a written product from the discussion that can be reviewed. The work we present aims to develop a framework for improving students' writing and study skills by making use of a variety of CMC tools. We report the preliminary results, which indicate ICT can improve some aspects of students' written debating skills. The transfer of these skills to more individual and reflective written work is currently being investigated.

We also discuss two other avenues of further work. The first continues to investigate the relationship between self-esteem, writing task and quality of writing. This addresses the question of whether raising self-esteem might be a mediating construct in improving performance. The second explores ways of providing support to literacy tutors to ensure that they, in turn, can help students to develop skills needed for online debate.

Research context

Chapeltown and Harehills Assisted Learning Computer School (CHALCS) is not a school but a community centre which supplements the tuition that students receive at their own schools. The centre has charitable status and receives funds from sources including the local authority and central government. CHALCS provides an environment for students to study out of school hours and is located in one of the poorest areas of Leeds: a district with high levels of unemployment. School truancy can result in many students performing well below their educational potential. Most CHALCS pupils are of African-Caribbean or South Asian ethnic origin and, for many, English is an additional language.

The Chapeltown and Harehills district of Leeds faces many of the problems often associated with inner-city ethnic minority areas. These problems can also be accompanied by high levels of drug abuse and crime. High disaffection and low expectation can further undermine educational goals and individual achievements (see http://www.chalcs.org.uk).

The centre was established in 1987 to combat problems of disaffection, low expectation and poor academic attainment. An evaluation project (Ravenscroft and Hartley 1998) showed that pupils attending CHALCS tend to obtain GCSE and A-Level results significantly higher than national and local averages. Furthermore, a CHALCS student moving on to higher education is generally offered a place at the institution of first choice.

Most students hear about CHALCS through 'word of mouth', although some may be referred by teachers. Attendance is voluntary but, as the centre has a long waiting list, tutors expect students to be committed to CHALCS classes. A separate project runs an 'Exclusion Programme' for those excluded from school; some of these pupils may also attend CHALCS classes.

CHALCS provides timetabled classes with formal tuition (not tied to National Curriculum), and open access sessions. The main study fields are maths, science and IT – primarily for students in school years 7–12 (pupils aged 11–18). A literacy programme also targets a younger age group aged 8–15 years. Open access sessions take place between 4–6 pm when pupils may use computers for homework or other educational activities. The average CHALCS class contains 14–18 students.

Computers are integral to the work of CHALCS. Computer facilities are provided not only to enable students to develop IT skills needed in the job market but also to support learning activities (Mohamed 1996) and enhance motivation (Cox 1997). A range of software is available and internet access is also provided.

The CHALCS literacy programme achieves good results with younger pupils. However, some older children risk falling further behind. They lack basic skills and confidence in writing to demonstrate the 'knowledge transformation skills' (Bereiter and Scardamalia 1987) demanded by the National Curriculum. It was, therefore, decided to design a new programme to target children in the 13–15 age group. The aim was to free them from the limitations of their basic skills to build confidence in writing and encourage the development of 'knowledge transformation'.

Related research

I Towards a model of developing writing

Writing involves a process of changing knowledge into text. Flower and Hayes (1980) see this as a problem involving many components: audience expectations, genre conventions and so on and argue that one characteristic of mature writers is their ability to solve this problem. According to Bereiter and Scardamalia (1987), as writers develop maturity they move from a process of 'knowledge telling' to one of 'knowledge transformation'. 'Knowledge telling' may be defined as the simple disgorging of everything a writer knows, whereas 'knowledge transformation' is the process of converting content into a text appropriate to context and audience by selecting and justifying relevant material, genre and structure. 'Knowledge' is defined by Bereiter and Scardamalia as being either 'structural knowledge' (of linguistic structures and strategies) or 'world knowledge' (of facts). The process of 'knowledge transformation' therefore involves developing structural knowledge and applying it to 'world knowledge'. The distinction Bereiter and Scardamalia make is based on a need to distinguish content or subject knowledge from writing knowledge. Both kinds of knowledge are composed of rich and overlapping schemata (see Kellogg, 1995 for an overview).

Schemata may be Concepts (serving to identify or categorize in the world), Frames (interpretations of relationships between such concepts e.g. objects in a scene) or Scripts (abstractions of experience that contain generalized procedures or rules used to capture knowledge of 'how to'). Schemata can be used to form unconscious expectations/predictions. In writing, as in all our cognitive life, we take information in through our senses (identifying what is present in the context). These interpretations then trigger schemata that categorize situations and events and trigger other schemata, many containing rules that generate internal and external responses. Together these schemata capture knowledge at varying levels of expertise.

Theories of scaffolding (Bruner 1978; Vygotsky 1978) suggest that developing writers can solve problems of transforming knowledge into text more easily working with a peer, than working alone. Exposure to peers' different experiences and approaches may help students assimilate new writing schemata or accommodate existing ones. This is borne out by Flower (1994) who shows how structured collaborative planning of written work can, by integrating social and instructional support, enable students to 'construct a robust strategy for being a constructive planner' (p. 143). Through collaboration, students can use more mature writing strategies and behaviours than those they can use working as individuals.

Burnett (1993) looks closely at the process of collaborative planning and believes collaboration succeeds only if certain pre-conditions are met. Tasks must be sufficiently difficult so that collaboration is genuinely necessary and students happy with the idea of working cooperatively. Students must be pre-prepared and tasks and groups carefully selected and structured to meet the needs of collaborative working. More importantly, Burnett argues that collaboration in writing is only effective when co-authors engage in 'substantive conflict' (arguing alternative points of view) rather than consensus.

2 Argument

When children start writing at school they are largely expected to write narrative, either factual or fictional (Andrews 1995). As their writing develops, they are also expected to demonstrate the skills of argumentative writing. However, from narrative to argument is not a clear progression and, as Andrews demonstrates, children need scaffolding to develop argumentative writing skills.

Kuhn et al. (1997) found that, after discussing opposing views in pairs, people were enabled to support ideas with more and better arguments. This confirms Burnett's findings that collaborative discussion (including 'substantive conflict') improved writing quality. Burnett (p. 134) identifies four types of decision-making:

1. Immediate agreement; that is, making an unelaborated decision about a single point.

2. Deferring consensus by elaborating a single point.
3. Deferring consensus by considering alternatives, which is one kind of substantive conflict.
4. Deferring consensus by voicing explicit disagreement, which is another kind of substantive conflict.

She claims that co-authors engaging in behaviours (3) and (4) produced better quality writing. Burnett's analysis can be criticized as simplistic because it allows only four options and does not accept that all these acts could occur within a single exchange. However, she makes an important observation about the need for constructive conflict: that simple agreement between co-authors does not produce collaboration that provides effective scaffolding of writing skills. Burnett's classification is supported by Mercer et al. (1999) who defined children's talk as 'exploratory', 'disputational' or 'cumulative' and concluded that 'exploratory talk' (involving active discussion of ideas) improved children's reasoning skills.

CMC supporting writing and argument

Studies on computer use in writing demonstrate that the technology can reduce writing apprehension and increase fluency (Neu and Scarcella 1990; Phinney 1990; Pennington 1996; Warschauer 1999). Pennington identified four improvement stages through computer-assisted writing: 'writing easier', 'writing more', 'writing differently' and 'writing better'. Most studies into computers and writing were carried out using word processing but some, such as Sullivan and Pratt (1996), Beauvois (1997) and Warschauer (1999) used synchronous CMC.

One claim for CMC is that it enables more equal participation in discussion (Sullivan and Pratt 1996; Warschauer 1996). In particular, Warschauer compared face-to-face and electronic discussion with racially mixed groups and found that ethnicity was a factor in limiting a student's face-to-face participation but did not restrict CMC engagement. In a mixed group such as a CHALCS class, this democratization could be significant.

Previous research suggests that CMC may encourage literacy skills development by increasing motivation to participate in text-based discussion (Sullivan and Pratt 1996; Warschauer 1999). A synchronous text-based CMC environment combines writing with discussion and can provide a rich setting for 'exploratory talk' and 'substantive conflict' as identified by Burnett (1993) and Mercer et al. (1999). This should lead to improved argumentation and reasoning skills.

Framework for the literacy programme

Following the hypothesis that text-based computer mediated discussion and assisted writing provides effective scaffolding of writing development, a new component of the CHALCS literacy programme was devised. This targets 11–15-year-olds, the group that appears to benefit least from existing provision. This programme, Discussion and Reporting Electronically (DaRE), broadly follows a writing process model (as described by Flower and Hayes 1981) that consists of the following phases:

- Group-based brain-storming of content ideas.
- Focused document structure planning; individual and group composition.
- Individual and group reflection on the process and product of writing.
- Synthesis of group ideas and the integration of critical feedback.
- Presentation of work to an identified audience.

Within DaRE these phases are incorporated into the following elements:

- Generation of topic themes via an asynchronous bulletin board.
- Synchronous text-based discussion of a topic.
- Collaborative planning and writing of a summary report.
- Presentation of report to the group.
- Receiving critical feedback from tutor and peers through bulletin board.
- Collaborative compilation of discussion summaries into class 'webzine' to be published on CHALCS public website for other pupils, parents and friends to read.

Pilot study

Research literature suggests that regular use of text-based synchronous CMC leads to:

- Increased fluency and confidence in writing. Phinney (1990)
- Increased ability to express written opinions clearly and articulately. Pennington (1996)
- Increased ability to develop and support arguments. Burnett (1993), Kuhn et al. (1997)
- enhanced awareness of audience and greater willingness to 'listen' to others. Warschauer (1999)

A small-scale study was devised within the DaRE context to determine the extent to which these benefits actually did accrue. The study used a synchronous bulletin board to start and conclude discussions with the main debate being conducted through the medium of synchronous online chat.

Method

WebCT, a web-based virtual learning environment, was installed at CHALCS. WebCT provides a range of tools for developing and managing learning programmes including the facility to display and link lecture notes; student grouping, tracking and management; a student project presentation 'area', testing and marking; email; bulletin boards and chat. The research study used the bulletin board and chat features together with a link to 'Yahooligans', a restricted internet search site for children. The classroom was arranged with computers in a double horseshoe formation. On occasion, when there were more students than available PCs, some students sat in another room, supervised by a teacher who did not participate in the discussions. Figure 5.1 shows the CHALCS classroom layout.

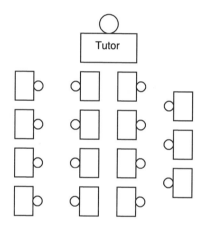

Figure 5.1 CHALCS classroom

Procedure

Each class lasted two hours and was led by a tutor from the CHALCS literacy team. At times a researcher there to observe, helped students who needed considerable support managing the technology. Occasionally the researcher joined discussions, taking the role of second tutor.

The first part of the session (usually one hour) was given over to CMC. The teacher had previously posted a discussion topic to the bulletin board. Topics were generally drawn from the students either by direct suggestion or emerging from the previous week's work. Students read the question and used chatrooms to discuss the topic. At the session's end each student composed and posted a reply to the bulletin board. The tutor read the chat-logs and bulletin board postings before posting a new discussion topic. The remainder of class time was used for other activities (not part of the study) such as reading comprehension, homework and practice for Key Stage 3 Assessments. These types of activity would have filled the entire session had CMC discussions not been introduced. In the final session, the tutor and students wrote informal evaluations of the programme on the bulletin board.

Please note that students' names have been changed to maintain anonymity.

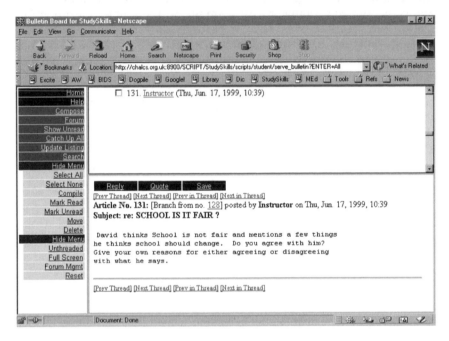

Figure 5.2   The bulletin board 'Starter'

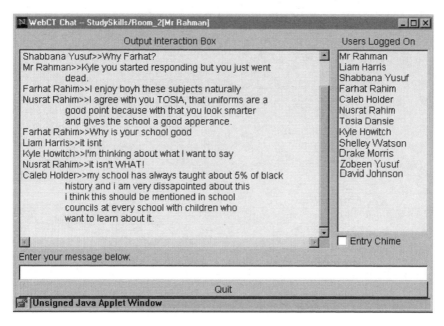

Figure 5.3 Chat tool in use

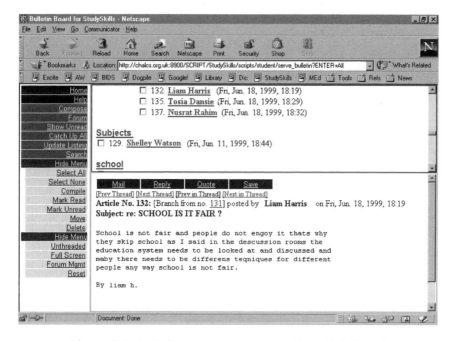

Figure 5.4 Post-discussion comments on the bulletin board

Participants and data collected

Nineteen children took part in the study: Figures 5.5 and 5.6 show the group's composition.

	Girls	Boys
Asian (Pakistani)	5	
West Indian	4	5
African	1	
Arabic		1
Arab/Asian		1
African/White		1
White	1	
Total	11	8

Figure 5.5   Study cohort by gender and ethnic group

School year (age)	Number of students
6 (10–11)	1
7 (11–12)	4
8 (12–13)	6
9 (13–14)	7
10 (14–15)	1

Figure 5.6   Ages of students in study cohort

The students were drawn from 11 local schools, with one pupil permanently excluded from school.

There were 12 logged chat sessions. Of these, six sessions (three before mid-term and three after mid-term) were analysed. The total number of words and turns in each session was counted and the average (mean) turn length calculated. Transcripts were also analysed to determine the percentage of turns containing material about the discussion topic and the percentage of turns containing reasoning or justification (indicated by the use of causal markers such as 'because' or 'so'). Figure 5.7 shows the data from the chat transcripts.

Topic		Words	Turns	Mean turn length	Turns on topic	Turns with reasons
30/4	Aliens	2021	373	5.41	21.4%	1.07%
7/5	Pop Music	1880	323	5.82	44%	4.02%
14/5	TV	831	219	3.79	78%	3.1%
18/6	Is School Fair?	1127	76	14.82	78.9%	22.3%
2/7	Women in Sport	883	75	11.77	93.3%	21.3%
9/7	Family Roles	1549	187	8.28	73.2%	11.7%

Figure 5.7 Results table 1

Overall results

Figure 5.7 suggests students' turns increased in length and complexity over time, indicating an increased fluency and confidence in writing. The word total increased and, as sessions progressed, there was also a trend towards fewer longer and more thoughtful turns. The table also suggests a shift from 'knowledge telling' to 'knowledge transformation' as students became more focused with less off-topic talk and more reasons given to support their views. There was also a shift in the type of topic chosen by students. In later sessions the topics selected seem more likely to prompt interesting debate. Taken together these results suggest an increased ability to develop and support arguments and a greater aware-ness of appropriate content and audience. In order to see if this was the case a more detailed qualitative analysis of contribution changes over time was necessary.

In early sessions, there were more turns in a discussion but these were significantly shorter than in later weeks. On 30/4 only 6.9 per cent of turns were more than 10 words long including only 0.5 per cent more than 20 words long. By 9/7, 23 per cent contained more than 10 words with 10.6 per cent more than 20 words long. During the same period the number of causal discourse markers (e.g. 'because' and 'so', typical of explaining and justifying) increased from just over 1 per cent on 30/4 to around 11 per cent on 9/7. This count of causal discourse markers was used to determine the number of turns containing reasons.

Qualitative discussion of results: topic selection and focus

In the earliest sessions, there were many more off-topic turns. Later, students selected topics that stimulated more debate and turns involved fuller reasoned arguments. For example 14/5 seemed to have many turns on topic although it is early in the programme, but analysis revealed most of these asked who liked a particular TV programme with few reasons given. Turns in later weeks tended to address each other's points more fully, suggesting improved sensitivity to the task-context and the need to justify and persuade.

53	Liam	Does anyone belive in alians
54	Tosia	i do since i seen you
55	Elodie	no i don't believe in aliens
56	Jabir	Aliens are little green men
57	Drake	Like Jabir
58	Tosia	you should know jabir

Figure 5.8   Poorly focused discussion from 30/4

183	Sahmeena	Drake what do you think should men only work and the women look after the house and children?
184	Drake	Men and women should be treated equally because it takes them both to make a waaaaaaaa!
185	David	I think the point in which everyboby is putting across is specifically on housework is very unfair, I honestly believe in equal oppertunities but it has already been clinically proven that women can do more things at once than men which means house work.
186	Mustafa	okay i'm off to reply
187	Sahmeena	whats waaaaaaaaaaaaaaaaaaaaaa
188	Shabbana	Men and women all have equal rights to anything done in a family house – hold. People say that a father is the head of the house but to me I think that the person who wrote that is not clever. This is because I feel that anyones mum and dad is the head of the house. I feel that mums and dads and children shoulld all become a team and do all the house work together. Not just the mum doing all the work.

Figure 5.9   More focused discussion from 9/7

There is a marked difference in the nature of off-topic turns when comparing early with later sessions. In early sessions, prolonged off-topic exchanges are commonplace, as in Figure 5.10. The topic is aliens but not only does this exchange bear no relation to the topic it also lacks coherence in the context of the debate.

29	Jabir	SO YOU THINK YOU ARE A RICK MAN
30	Elodie	drake your sad MAN!
31	Drake	Nuff respect to DMX Ruff Ryders
32	Tosia	What the heck is a rick man
33	Drake	Wobble Wobble
34	Elodie	easi drake ruff ryders are RUFF. p.s your lip drake

Figure 5.10   Typical off-topic exchange on 30/4

In later sessions, off-topic exchanges are rare and off-topic turns more likely to be brief digressions as in Figure 5.11 where Shabbana is correcting the spelling of her name.

189	Sahmeena	good point shabanna
190	Caleb	sorry. where would a man be without a woman.
191	Shabbana	Sahmeena its SHABBANA

Figure 5.11   Off-topic turn from 9/7

In earlier sessions points were raised through simple questions and answered without elaboration (Figure 5.12). As the programme progressed students were more likely to refer to and comment on each other's points and ask questions that extended the scope of discussion. In Figure 5.13, for example, David echoes and elaborates a point made by Liam before raising a new question.

70	Tosia	My fav comedys are sister sister, smart guy, moesha, most of those shows come on cable though. I like them because there funny.
71	Caresse	me too
72	Dexter	I think sister sister is the best

Figure 5.12   Simple answers to a simple question on 14/5

27	David	On the point of womens football that Liam made it will be very rare that you will here about the womens World Cup because at this time of year you will have Wimbledon, World Cup cricket as well as Test match cricket on TV, and mostly mens sport will have better TV coverage than the womens game because most women aren't interested in sport except in athletics, anyway whats your opinion on womens athletics.

Figure 5.13   Addressing and extending a point on 2/7

Making and backing points: towards a more reasoned debate

In Figure 5.14, Drake describes what he would do if he met an alien. Although technically on-topic, his remark does not further the debate, especially as he does not elaborate his views in subsequent remarks. Figure 5.15, however, shows Drake adding substantially to discussion with a contribution showing he has thought about what other people said, can evaluate their comments and put forward his own reasoned opinions.

---

11   Drake   I would stab it, shoot it, blow it up, and then bun a big fat juicy spliff

---

Figure 5.14   On topic but not advancing the debate (30/4)

---

13   Drake   I agree with David in the Black department but the uniform bit don't even go there. If people were so bothered about what school they could just ask it's like the only reason we have to wear the school uniform is to show peole what school we go to. There should at least be a seperate class for seperate people who want to learn about thier black roots. It would be good to be able to learn this so in the future we can say this school has taught me this.

Figure 5.15   Complex, transformational writing (18/6)

A similar development can be seen in Shabbana's contributions on 14/5 and 9/7 (Figures 5.16 and 5.9). In the earlier session Shabbana expresses an opinion but no further information, even about the genres to which her favourite programmes belong. Her contribution on 9/7 (Figure 5.9) is elaborated; she explains the context of her opinion and is willing to argue her viewpoint.

---

146   Shabbana   MY FAVOURITE PROGRAMMES ON ZEE ARE AMMANAT, HASRATEIN AND ZEE TOP 10

Figure 5.16   Unelaborated opinion on 14/5

Unlike many students, Tosia could substantiate her opinions in the early weeks of the programme. Even so, her ability to elaborate her views improved as Figures 5.17 and 5.18 show.

---

83   Tosia   Another comedy I like is The Fresh Prince of Bel Air because I like the characters, they are all funny in their own way. Hilery is funny because sh's dumb and Carlton is funny because he hates Will.

Figure 5.17   Tosia's reasoned opinion on 14/5

| 17 | Tosia | I don't think there is anything wrong with wearing scholl uniform because if you wear your own clothes to school some people might diss you about the clothes you wear so if you wear school uniform everyone is wearing the same thing. I think my school uniform is okay because it doesn't stand out that much. |

Figure 5.18   Tosia's reasoned opinion on 18/6

The topic discussed on 18/6 ('Is School Fair?') made it easier to find effective arguments. However, the selection of topics itself was something that developed during the programme. Figure 5.17 also demonstrates it was possible to put forward reasoned opinions even with the less complex topics of the early weeks; that Tosia was the only student to do this, demonstrates the extent to which the other class members improved as the programme progressed.

Some topics recurred in the programme's second phase but framed in ways that prompted more focused discussion. For example, Sahmeena suggested music and films but not simply what music and films people liked. She wrote the following questions asking for explicit comparison and contrast: 'Indian songs and movies or English songs and movies? Which do you prefer? Indian or English?? Which drives you nuts and which do you want on??'

Changes in attitude: becoming more constructive and less destructive

Before the programme the tutor rated Drake as unmotivated and childish in class. Afterwards the tutor remarked on the apparent increase in maturity. As Figures 5.14 and 5.19 show, in the early weeks, Drake's behaviour in discussion rarely advanced the debate and could be destructive, even offensive. In later sessions, Drake's behaviour was generally constructive (as in Figure 5.15) and when he made jokey contributions they were within the debate framework and contributed to the discussion (Figure 5.20).

| 75 | Drake | Liam has only got a Barbie Doll |
| 76 | Drake | With a hole |

Figure 5.19   Offensive behaviour on 30/4

| 46 | Drake | Women make tennis look much more better. he he he heee! |

Figure 5.20   Constructive joke on 2/7

Liam also changed in attitude and behaviour. The tutor commented that, before the programme, Liam was often sarcastic and tended to incite trouble. Three months after the programme finished the tutor observed Liam was more organized and wanted to do more work (to prove he could do better than David). Liam was less sarcastic and tended to take people more seriously.

45	Liam	Drake I can smell your B.O from here

Figure 5.21   Inciting conflict on 30/4

6	Liam	I think women should have the same rights and pay as men. OK then lets take the womens world cup in America we havent heard eanything really about it only that england dident make it becauce the coaching for womans is as noot as high a standard as mens football. I also agree with daved that womens games are much better than mens. !!!!!!!!!!!!!!!!!!!!

Figure 5.22   Constructive contribution on 2/7

Inclusiveness of discussion

WebCT's 'chat' feature has four 'rooms' and one striking feature of online debates in early weeks was that students tended to divide into two groups. One group mainly consisted of boys with the Black and White girls whilst the other group contained girls, mainly Asian. The 'girls' group' appeared quite possessive of their 'space'. For example, in Figure 5.23, the Asian girls are aware that Shelley (a white girl) has joined them and, initially, are guarded, although they go on to include her in their conversation.

50	Zobeen	Shelley has entered
51	Farhat	ARE YOU GOING TO WATCH THE MOVIE TONIGHT
52	Zobeen	Maybe Farhat
53	Shabbana	SHELEY I DON'T THINK YOU UNDERSTAND WHATT
54	Farhat	WHY ARE YOU WATCHING ANYTHING ELSE
55	Shabbana	WE ARE TALKING ABOUT
56	Zobeen	Shelley what do you like

Figure 5.23   Reaction to a 'newcomer' 7/5

In later sessions, all students used the same room. There was still a slight tendency for some, especially Farhat, Sahmeena, Zobeen, and Shabbana (who share a family relationship) to talk mainly to each other. Figure 5.24

24	Shabbana	What is your fav subject Farhat?
25	Farhat	My favourite subject is mathematics and technology.
26	Shabbana	Why Farhat?
12	Sahmeena	The question that has to be answered is 'who should look after the family'? What do you think faz?

Figure 5.24 Examples of 'exclusive' communication from 18/6 and 9/7

shows two examples of these students directing questions to each other. There was no reason why these questions could not be asked to the whole group.

In later sessions there are far more examples of 'inclusive' talk, where students respond to each other, commenting on opinions or asking each other's views.

38	David	... I also definitly disagree with Shabbana
57	Aliza	mostafa do you think that men and women should do things equal
58	Mustafa	you can say that again
66	Aliza	tosia i agree
67	Mustafa	I don't. Women should be at home for the men
92	Tosia	I partly agree with Shelley ...
150	Sahmeena	ARE YOU AWAKE CALEB
151	Shabbana	Zobeen what does your dad work as?!!!!!
152	Caleb	i think this no
158	Tosia	I think people like Mustafa should keep their opinions to their self because they are living in the past and nobody agrees with them.
159	Sahmeena	Caleb what do you think?

Figure 5.25 'Inclusive' communication from 9/7

Affirming and encouraging others

As the discussion programme progressed students revealed greater respect for other people and their opinions. In earlier sessions students dismissed each other's contributions if they did not agree with them. Sometimes this could be creative as in Figure 5.27 where repeated 'z's' expressed disdainfully the view that jazz was boring. More commonly, however, disagreement was expressed through personal insult as in Figures 5.26 and 5.28.

159	Paula	Sahmeena you must be mental

Figure 5.26 Disagreement 30/5

17	Jabir	Rap IS not just bad music it is crazy mans music
18	Mustafa	why do you like JAZZZZZZZZZ I think it's rubbish
19	Drake	raps got more listeners than jazzzzzzzzzzzzzzzzzzzzzzzzzzzzzzzzzz
20	David	Drake, Tell that Jabir to stop talking about jazzzzzzzzzzzzzzzz!

Figure 5.27 Disagreement 7/5

190	Farhat	YOU ARE SAD

Figure 5.28 Disagreement 14/5

In later sessions disagreement occurred less often, but when it did was more likely to be expressed explicitly and with a considered challenge to the other person's statement.

74	Nusrat	At some school we do learn about the black history, but we have to keep in mind that we are being taught in a british society, which may make a difference to what we are taught.
78	Caleb	well nusrat what does that mean because there are lots of black people in britain

Figure 5.29 Disagreement 18/6

40	David	I disagree in the fact of Dexter going on about uneven pay, women should get the same pay as men when they play the certain sporting activity to the same distance as men.

Figure 5.30 Disagreement 2/7

On 9/7 Mustafa remarked 'women should be at home for the men'. As Figure 5.31 shows, this provoked considerable disagreement. However, there are no unreasoned insults such as those that appeared in earlier sessions. Instead there are arguments that

1. times have changed;
2. women and men should be equal (a functional argument as classified by Kuhn et al. (1997);
3. women will not want to marry a man who thinks that women should stay at home (functional);
4. in real life families women do not stay at home.

78	Tosia	Mustafa is living in the past. Things have changed Mustafa. Wake Up!!!
88	Liam	womenand men should be equal and should not be (at home waiting for the man) as Mustafa said
101	David	Mustafa do you intend to have a job and a wife when you're older or are you going to carry on being sexist?
128	David	Mustafa do you live in the kind of family you are advertiving 'Where the women cleans the house and the man goes out to work'.

Figure 5.31 Disagreement 9/7

Figure 5.32 shows different patterns of insults (including aggressive phrases such as 'I will knock you out . . .'), disagreements and agreement (signalled by phrases such as 'I agree'). The table shows both numbers of turns containing those elements and those turns as percentages of the total turns in that session. The differences in the other weeks are less marked but still show that the students were more likely to challenge than to insult.

Week	Total turns	Insults/aggression/ Offensive language	Simple disagreement	Argument/ challenge	Explicit agreement
30/4	373	36 (9.6%)	0	0	3 (0.8%)
9/7	187	2 (1%)	3 (1.6%)	15 (8%)	10 (5.3%)

Figure 5.32 Types of agreement/disagreement in early and late stages of the programme

Figure 5.32 shows that students were more likely to affirm each other's points through explicit agreement in later sessions. There was little explicit encouragement of the 'X made a good point' type. It should be noted, though, that preliminary results from the study's next stage show that appropriate modelling of such behaviour by the tutor quickly leads to students adopting explicit peer validation.

Discussion of results

The most striking evidence from the online chat session shows that students' 'chat' writing increased in length and complexity and revealed more 'knowledge transformation' over time as they:

- selected topics that prompted more debate;
- addressed each other's comments more;
- became more focused and reasoned – more 'on topic';
- supported their opinions with more detailed arguments;
- engaged in more substantive conflict;
- debated points of disagreement instead of insulting each other.

Topics suggested for discussion became more sophisticated during the programme; early topics included pop music and favourite TV programmes, whereas later topics included fairness in schools and equality in the family. The later topics may have helped facilitate more complex discussion but there was also an improvement in the students' abilities (evidenced by the contrast between the performance of Tosia, a particularly able child, and others during the early sessions).

In the early stages of chat much reasoning was descriptive, indicating students were working from a 'knowledge telling' model of writing. As the chat progressed, arguments became more complex, possibly indicating an increased maturity leading to the emergence of 'knowledge transformation' whereby writers become more selective of content and presentation. Students recognized the need to communicate effectively their own ideas and opinions to the group to further debate, and tried to ensure that those views were supported by evidence. Furthermore, in later weeks students were willing to challenge those opinions unsustained by evidence (as opposed to simple disagreement). This indicates a move from simple agreement or unsubstantiated disagreement towards the 'substantive conflict' that Burnett (1993)described as essential for effective use of collaboration in scaffolding writing. The detailed challenges to arguments (and echoing of other people's points) also shows that students were 'listening' more effectively to each other. That students were aware of this process is supported by the evaluations in which some commented that they had learned to pay attention to other peoples' opinions and to see matters from other points of view. The chat became more evenly distributed and disruptive students became more constructive. Over time the chat also became more inclusive as participants encouraged each other to contribute, gave more positive feedback and learned to challenge other's viewpoints rather than disagree with insults or aggression.

In Pennington's terms students were 'Writing Easier, Writing More and Writing Differently' (Pennington 1996). Some students, such as Tosia, had these skills from the outset, others, like Drake, developed them during the programme. This suggests that they were increasing in confidence: both in the belief they had something which was worth saying and in their abilities to write it coherently. This is supported by students' own evaluations in which some pupils commented that they had become more confident as a result of the CMC.

The tutor believed the chat helped students take more care with spelling and grammar. Online chat is not a medium which facilitates correct spelling. There is no spell-checker and the need to respond quickly means that typing errors are frequent. However, students often challenged each other's spelling, sometimes because inaccurate spelling made it difficult to understand something a student 'said' whilst sometimes the challenge seemed to be a form of teasing. The tutor believed the challenges encouraged students to think more about making their writing understandable. This suggests a developing awareness of audience.

Limitations of the study

This research study was limited in that it dealt with a single group of students and, due to the constraints of the CHALCS context, not all students attended classes regularly. Therefore the performances of some students did not change to the same extent as those who attended more regularly. Furthermore, whereas online behaviour of regular attenders changed as the study progressed, irregular attenders tended to exhibit the same behaviour patterns in later sessions as they had done in earlier ones. This was potentially disruptive to the group as a whole.

The role of the teacher changed during the study, as he and the students became more accustomed to the technology. Early on, students needed considerable assistance with logging on to the chat. When the group was at full strength, there were not enough computers for all and furthermore, several computers did not work. Because of this, in some sessions, considerable tutor and pupil time was wasted in finding working computers, with some students being moved to a separate room. This was worse in early sessions. This meant that some pupil performances were under-represented in particular sessions; although a pupil might have been physically present, he or she might not have accessed the chat until late in the session. The changing role of tutor could be seen from the fact that, although he was usually present online during a session, he was able to make a greater contribution to later chats and this may have influenced the behaviour of students. Harwood (1995) found that when a teacher was present in the interaction, pupils were more likely to sustain a discussion thread and justify opinions.

As the CMC programme was an addition to an existing course and intended to develop process skills rather than teach content, the tutor spent relatively little time on preparation and did not comment on or correct students' contributions (after the end of the session). In another setting, with more focus on content, the teacher could spend more time collecting websites (or other resources) for students to gather information before the discussion. The teacher might also give feedback to students on their bulletin board contributions or take examples from their writing for teaching language points. How much preparation or feedback is needed depends on the context in which the lesson is planned, its aims and objectives.

One problem was the use of private messages. Students were never taught how to send private messages to each other but they quickly acquired the skill. Private messages are not logged, indeed, WebCT does not even record the fact that a private message has been sent, which means that research data may be lost. Furthermore, the non-recording of private messages makes it difficult for teachers to control or prevent the sending of abusive or inappropriate messages. This point has been made to WebCT designers. As this environment was created originally for university students, the designers had not considered that younger teenagers might be less mature in their use of the technology. The content of the first session, when students had not realized that the discussions were logged (although they were informed), showed that some group members will send offensive messages to each other if they think they can get away with it. For this reason the tutor prohibited the sending of private messages and enforced this by occasionally patrolling the classroom. The fact that the sending of private messages was possible (and did happen, especially in the early stages) means that some of the chat-log data might not be complete.

Conclusions and future work

This small-scale study was carried out to evaluate the use of CMC chat with students aged 11–14 years within the context of an out-of-school programme to reduce the literacy deficit suffered by many inner-city pupils. The results indicated that the chat enabled students to choose and debate more complex topics and focus more during discussions. They were more likely to justify their own opinions and to make reasoned challenges to opposing points of view. They also showed more respect for each other. There was an improvement in students' ability to construct and put forward detailed arguments, revealing a move from knowledge telling to knowledge transformation.

Although in their evaluations of the CMC programme some students said they were more confident about writing, the hypothesis that writing anxiety is reduced by chat requires further study. The tutor believed the chat helped students take more care with spelling and grammar; this also requires further objective analysis. More detailed and systematic research must be carried through using a self-esteem attitude scale with a more detailed analysis of chat-logs to track the development of individual students during the programme. There should also be pre and post testing of students' written work in other contexts to determine the extent to which skills developed through the programme may be transferred to other situations.

Synchronous online chat is informal and does not require participants to write extended texts. Indeed, extended writing tends to be discouraged by other participants as it takes too much time to read and digest. Therefore the full DaRE programme aims to enable students to transfer their new skills to other writing contexts by including collaborative report writing and presentation (using a formal word processing tool shared through applications such as NetMeeting).

The tutor's role within debate needs further research, particularly the effect that the tutor's behaviour has upon other participants. Ways of providing additional support to the scaffolding process by which the tutor models desired behaviour and gradually fades from the process are being investigated through the development of a framework for facilitating online debate. This is necessary for several reasons. First, some students may have participated in internet chat within other contexts, for example recreational chat websites such as TeenChat and need support to make the cultural shift to structured debate. Second, some students may be able to articulate their views in oral debate but may need scaffolding to transfer these skills to the medium of synchronous text-based discussion. Finally, some students may lack debating skills and need support to develop techniques such as elaboration, justification, questioning or encouraging other group members.

Acknowledgements

Work reported here was part funded by an ESRC CASE Research Studentship in collaboration with Chapeltown and Harehills Assisted Learning Computer School (CHALCS). The authors particularly thank Mr Brainard Braimah (Director CHALCS), Mr Abdul Jalloh (Literacy Tutor CHALCS).

References

Andrews, R. (1995) *Teaching and Learning Argument*. London: Cassell.
Beauvois, M.H. (1997) High-tech, high-touch: from discussion to composition in the networked classroom, *Computer-Assisted Language Learning*, 10(1): 57–69.

Bereiter, C. and Scardamalia, M. (1987) *The Psychology of Written Composition*. Hillsdale, NJ: Lawrence Erlbaum and Associates.

Burnett, R.E. (1993) Decision-making during the collaborative planning of coauthors, in A. Penrose, and B. Sitko (eds) *Hearing Ourselves Think: Cognitive Research in the College Writing Classroom*. Oxford: Oxford University Press.

Cox, M. (1997) *The Effects of Information Technology on Students' Motivation*, Summary report. London: King's College London/NCET.

Flower, L. (1994) *The Construction of Negotiated Meaning: A Social Cognitive Theory of Writing*. Carbondale, Illinois: Southern Illinois University Press.

Flower, L.S. and Hayes, J.R. (1980) The dynamics of composing: making plans and juggling constraints, in L. Gregg and R. Steinberg (eds) *Cognitive Processes in Writing*. Hillsdale, NJ: Erlbaum.

Flower, L.S. and Hayes, J.R. (1981) A cognitive process theory of writing, *College Composition and Communication*, 32: 365–87.

Harwood, D. (1995) The pedagogy of the world studies, 8–13 Project: the influence of the presence/absence of the teacher upon primary children's collaborative group work, *British Educational Research Journal*, 21(5): 587–611.

Kellogg, R.T. (1995) *Cognitive Psychology*. London: Sage Publications.

Kuhn, D., Shaw, V. and Felton, M. (1997) Effects of dyadic interaction on argumentative reasoning, *Cognition and Instruction*, 15(3): 287–315.

Mercer, N., Wegerif, R. and Dawes, L. (1999) Children's talk and the development of reasoning in the classroom, *British Educational Research Journal*, 25(1): 95–111.

Mohamed, Z.B. (1996) An evaluation of a extra-school science programme in a multi-ethnic community: a computer-based case study. Unpublished PhD thesis, University of Leeds.

Neu, J. and Scarcella, R. (1990) Word processing in the ESL writing classroom: a survey of student attitudes, in P. Dunkel (ed.) *Computer Assisted Language Learning and Testing*. New York: Newbury House.

Pennington, M. (1996) Writing the natural way: on Computer, *Computer Assisted Language Learning*, 9: 2–3.

Phinney, M. (1990) Computer-assisted writing and writing apprehension in ESL students, in P. Dunkel (ed.) *Computer Assisted Language Learning and Testing*. New York: Newbury House.

Ravenscroft, A. and Hartley, R. (1998) *Evaluation of Chapeltown and Harehills Assisted Learning Computer School (CHALCS)*. Leeds: Computer Based Learning Unit, University of Leeds.

Sullivan, N. and Pratt, E. (1996) A comparative study of two ESL writing environments: a computer-assisted classroom and a traditional oral classroom, *System*, 29(4): 491–501.

Vygotsky, L.S. (1978) *Mind in Society: The Development of Higher Psychological Processes*. Cambridge, Mass: Harvard University Press.

Walker, S.A. and Pilkington, R.M. (2000) Networked communication and the collaborative development of written expression at Key Stage Three. Paper presented to the Second International Conference on Networked Learning, Lancaster, 17–19 April.

Warschauer, M. (1996) Comparing face-to-face and electronic discussion in the second language classroom, *CALICO Journal*, 13(2): 7–26.

Warschauer, M. (1999) *Electronic Literacies*. Mahwah, New Jersey: Erlbaum.
Warcshauer, M., Turbee, L. and Roberts, B. (1996) Computer learning networks and student empowerment, *System*, 24(1): 1–14.

CHALCS http://www.chalcs.org.uk
TeenChat http://www.teenchat.com
WebCT http://www.webct.com/
Yahooligans http://www.yahooligans.com

6

ICT AND THE LITERACY PRACTICES OF STUDENT WRITING

Charles Crook and Roy Dymott

The twin concerns of this chapter may each seem to have a circumscribed quality. Writing is surely something sufficiently clear that we can spot it when it is in progress. For example, if some friend wanted a photograph of 'you writing', it would be easy to supply a convincing image. Similarly, ICT is easy to spot. Typically, it is identified with the material form of the desktop computer. This technology has the appearance of a self-contained object. Such circumscribed characteristics of ICT and of writing might encourage a slippage in conceptual vocabulary. It becomes natural to conceptualize writing as a kind of *behaviour*. It becomes easy to conceptualize the computer as a kind of *stimulus*, a tool-to-hand. Perhaps such a perspective cultivates the belief that research questions about 'the effects of ICT on writing' are straightforward. We argue that they are not.

Neither item in this ICT/writing relationship has such a singular identity. Consider the text you are currently reading. Composing the preceding paragraph certainly involved keyboard tapping and screen staring: activities that perhaps could be photographed as 'me writing'. However, much more was involved than those simple behaviours. There was the business of distributing attention. This applies to the screen, the keyboard, and a set of paper notes. But also – because of a social interruption – it applies to the screen and other forms of event on the periphery. Writing is organized (it is located and scheduled) to be in a useful harmony with this periphery: sometimes exploiting it, sometimes needing to be insulated from it. There is a place and time for this keyboard tapping. In the present case, my site-for-writing conveys a sense of design, or intentionality. The place is one arranged to best orchestrate the management of certain material resources, and to filter out events that are thought to be distracting. In addition to this physical context, writing involves a framework of more abstract constraints associated with the task: for example, matters of deadlines, publishers, editors and audience. All these are built into the organization of what gets done, including the various supporting technologies. Finally, the present piece of writing is *co*-authored: a circumstance that clearly disturbs any orderliness in our photographic capture of writing-in-progress.

Thus, our first point is that writing cannot be circumscribed in the convenient manner that might support simple research designs. Instead, writing seems to confront us with a rich *system* of activities. Individuals will realize these in different ways, depending on their histories of enculturation. Indeed, 'cultural practice' may be the best way to characterize the achievement of writing. Our second point concerns how best to conceptualize the writing/technology *relationship*. Here we propose that they are mutually constitutive. Again, this captures the sense in which the second term in our interest – 'computers' – cannot be any more easily circumscribed than 'writing'. Computers (and all their infrastructures) are inert pieces of material, at least until drawn into forms of human activity. If we sometimes identify 'properties of the technology', this is because we have noted something orderly about its appropriation into an activity system where we find it operating. Similarly, if we refer to 'properties of writing', it is because some author is acting in an organized way *with* technology – ICT perhaps, but a wide range of other technologies could be implicated. Thus, these items are inherently interdependent.

Such a conceptual framework is readily derived from cultural psychology (Cole 1996). Study of activity in cultural psychological terms entails adopting as an analytic unit not the traditional 'individual' of mainstream psychology, but the 'individual-acting-with-mediational-means'. That is, psychological phenomena are everywhere seen to entail activity mediated by some cultural resource or other – an artefact, technology, symbol system, social practice etc. Unlike the *im*-mediate behaviour of other species, the activity of human beings involves engagement with a material and social world through the intervention of these cultural resources. This invites an analysis of human action that stresses its inherent embeddedness in culture. Here we address one particular mutual engagement with culture, one concerning the inter-penetration of writing and new technology. In adopting a cultural perspective, we are anxious to resist simple formulations that appeal to 'the effects of ICT on writing'. Yet we are aware that new technologies are deeply implicated in the writing practices of many authors. The nature of that relationship demands some form of rigorous understanding. The challenge, therefore, is to capture as honestly as possible the relevant dynamic.

So far, our analytic preference has been presented in rather abstract terms. It may be useful to invoke a more concrete example offering an accessible analogy. In discussing mediation and its effects, Cole and Griffen (1980) seek a simple parallel for probing the way we speak about the influence of modern technologies that support cognition. They note it is tempting to describe such tools in terms of 'cognitive amplifiers'. In the present context, some may wish to consider ICT as amplifying the power of writers. However, this may be misleading – both in terms of how it conceptualizes the underlying activity (writing) and how it conceptualizes the impact of the technology (amplifying).

To pursue their concern about amplification, Cole and Griffen offer an analysis (somewhat macabre) of the social practice of hunting and killing. They invite us to imagine a traditional society in which prey are captured and killed with simple weapons. Visitors from some modern society furnish these traditional people with guns – a new mediational means to enter their system of hunting. More animals are killed in shorter periods. Accordingly, we might say that the guns served to 'amplify' killing. Just as we might say that computers amplify the more cognitive enterprises of calculating, writing, or whatever. If all we mean by amplifying an activity is an increase in output – for example, more animals getting killed – then this seems an innocent enough way of talking. However, it is less obvious that the hunter's capacity to kill has been 'amplified' when the new weapon is not to hand. What has been changed by the technology is not some property of the individual but the manner in which some activity can be carried out – when the technology is available.

The example sharpens our sensitivity to the three issues at stake here – writing (cf. killing), ICT (cf. guns) and re-mediation (new technologies entering existing cultural practices). First, killing, like writing, is no rigidly defined pattern of behaviour. It involves practices of social coordination, such as gathering, stalking and ambushing as well as recovery, distribution, honour and so on. In short, the human action invoked in these relationships has a systemic character. Second, the technologies involved are similarly complex. Guns are not artefacts with some singular nature. They derive whatever properties are ascribed to them from how they enter into cultural practices. A gun is different according to it being a starting pistol, a rescue flare, a fairground challenge, or a hunting weapon. Its identity is constituted by the systems of activity with which it is involved. Finally, the parallel encourages us to notice how the relationship between such activity systems and technologies is itself complex. It is a relationship of re-configuration, not enhancement. Killing is not amplified by new technology. Re-mediation involves not so much amplification of some activity as changing the manner in which it is organized or exercised. Guns arrive: the hunting is done differently. ICT arrives: the writing is done differently.

This argument, well developed by Bruce (1997), denies the value of conceptualizing writing and technology in terms of 'separate realms'. Yet examples are needed to reinforce this analysis of writing. We develop a particular example here. We have chosen the case of *undergraduate writing*. It is authentic, richly-structured and accessible to research. Our aim is to reveal the sense in which it is an activity system: that is, individuals co-ordinating with a variety of cultural supports in the interests of producing text. Our particular interest is in positioning the resource of ICT as a developing influence within such systems of activity. Research on ICT and writing tends to dwell upon word processors: how their design re-mediates composition. Yet increasing use of this one particular technical tool does not suddenly identify writing as being now 'about' computer technology or now 'effected by' computer technology. Writing has always entailed an activity engaged with technologies: pens and paper but also a range of other cultural resources that frame up what we do when we say we write. The undergraduate example should illustrate this well. The particular case of ICT represents clearly the richly mediated nature of this activity.

First we provide a general introduction to the circumstances of undergraduate writing as a useful model system. Then we discuss five topics involving the intrusion of ICT into writing. We suggest that each furnishes a useful focal point for research. Not that this list is intended to be exhaustive. The aim is not to partition the domain of interest into five comprehensive areas identifying five separate independent variables for researchers to study. Any comparative analysis provoked by this conceptual organization is not in the spirit of evaluating 'effects'. Rather, it creates a device for revealing the structure of the underlying practice, a structure that might otherwise be hidden from view by virtue of its familiarity. We do this

a) in relation to the physicality of writing and text: considering the ICT context of writing on a screen;
b) we consider how writing is shaped by a technology connected to a network of other computers and computer users;
c) we discuss text as traffic within a community infrastructure of ICT;
d) we consider text in relation to audience and the role of ICT in that relationship;
e) writing is located within a social context of appraisal and evaluation.

Studying undergraduate writing

The assumption that writing and ICT describe separate realms encourages a particular form of experimentation. Teachers and researchers alike ask what effects technologies have on literacy practices which are viewed as skills that might be isolated from the peculiarities of their situation. Accordingly, experiments are conducted that attempt such isolation. An experimental task might be designed to embody a specific literacy skill (or subset of skills). The task then isolates this skill from others, and from the material conditions of everyday literacy, so that technology's 'effects' upon it can be established. This is most clearly seen in the way in which the experimental research literature separates reading and writing. Experimental reading tasks almost never involve participants in any act of writing (see Dillon (1992) for a literature review). And although experimental writing tasks unavoidably involve writers in reading their own texts, the separation between reading and writing is achieved as far as possible by excluding the use of source texts from the task (see Ransdell and Levy (1994) for a partial review). Under this approach attention is heavily focused upon outcomes with relatively little concern for processes. If processes are investigated, it is typically with the aim of establishing how technologies change the frequency and sequence of those with an abstract and immutable quality – such as Hayes and Flower's (1980) processes of generating, organizing and translating ideas (for example, Kellogg and Mueller 1993). This approach has made only modest progress and generated some inconsistent findings (Bruce 1997).

The assumption that literacy practices are comprised of abstract skills that can be studied in isolation from the peculiarities of the situation (including writing tools) and in isolation from each other is problematic. In a review of the experimental literature comparing reading from paper and reading from VDUs, Dillon (1990: 1322) notes:

> One is struck in reviewing this literature by the rather limited and often distorted view of reading that ergonomists seem to have. Most seem to concern themselves with the control of so many variables that the resulting experimental task bears little resemblance to the activities most of us routinely perform as 'reading'.

Equivalent criticism could equally be applied to the experimental literature on writing. An experimental writing task typically involves composing a short text, in a single session, in the absence of source documents (Snyder 1993) and, as noted by Torrance (1996), often in an unfamiliar genre.

Authentic literacy practices that occur outside the laboratory bear only slight resemblance to the isolated, sparsely resourced, tasks enacted inside it. The undergraduate coursework essay writer is embedded in rich contexts; including material artefacts such as, journals, books, computers, and the internet. The student may also fashion additional resources such as lecture notes, notes from reading, written outlines, and drafts. In a study of genuine coursework essay production (Dymott and Crook 2001a), mediation by such materials was a pervasive feature of coursework essay production. Great diversity was found across individuals in terms of the form taken by mediated activity. This mediation was sufficiently strong, and constitutive of sufficiently diverse forms of practice, as to call into question the validity of even apparently basic distinctions between literacy 'skills', such as between note-taking and drafting. The inability to find a mapping between authentic, richly mediated literacy activity and the literacy skills investigated in the lab should lead us to question the applicability of laboratory findings to authentic activity, and perhaps to question the value of the notion of generic, context independent literacy skills.

In the following sections, we draw upon our own research to pursue these reservations and to locate them in relation to new technologies. Generally our research involved the study of students working under natural conditions of writing and assessment. We invited them to keep detailed diaries, interviewed them, and logged the manner in which they use their personal ICT resources. In some cases, we saw an advantage in a more controlled form of study: one in which two different circumstances for writing are observed and compared. In such cases we wished to protect the authentic goals and motives of participants: involving them with genre of composition they recognize. Such an orchestrated research contrast between two mediational means for writing can remain useful. It can be a device for exposing the significance of some otherwise concealed dimension of the writing situation. In fact, this strategy is illustrated in the next section, where we dwell upon the materiality of writing – as accessed by consideration of how screen-based composition re-mediates what gets done.

A general caution is necessary. The position we adopted can create problems with our vocabulary for talking about 'writing' here. We urge that it not be considered in so circumscribed a way that we fail to pursue the rich mediational framework in which it is set. The very term 'writing' should orient us towards a complex activity system and not constrain us only to consider the canonical image of exercising pen-and-paper or keyboard-and-screen. Yet in doing the work of analysis, it may often be necessary to refer to some constituent component of an activity system. In particular, it may be necessary to refer specifically to the mechanics of using pen or keyboard. Accordingly, in some of what follows we may sometimes choose to make 'writing' refer to the local circumstances of generating text – momentary actions with pen, keys or whatever.

1. Text on the screen

The physical qualities of on-screen text are clearly different from those of text on paper. These differences have significance for readers' and writers' experiences of text. We have investigated students' activity as they composed short essays; once from sources presented on A4 paper, and once from sources presented on a computer screen (Dymott and Crook 2001 [b]). The computer screen constituted a smaller working space than the physical desk top. Accordingly, while whole pages of *paper* text would be made visible at any one time, the screen typically displayed much less than a single page. The participants in our observations often laid out paper so that more than one document was visible at any time. Only one participant attempted this with on-screen texts, and accomplished it only with great difficulty. Indeed, most manipulations of documents were more readily performed on paper than on screen: paper offered a far more 'direct' (Hutchins, Hollan and Norman 1986) form of manipulation. Scrolling within a document typically involved a pause in reading while visual attention was shifted to an on-screen scroll bar. Yet the tactile properties of pages meant that they could be turned without distracting visual attention from reading. Numerous such differences between paper and screen have been associated with different experiences of paper and computer texts in both laboratory studies (Hansen and Haas 1988) and anecdotal reports (Chandler 1995). One of the more reliable findings from all lines of research is that users of on-screen writing have greater difficulty apprehending a document's global structure or developing what Hansen and Haas (1988) call a 'sense of text' – a *'grasp of the structural and semantic arrangement of the text – the absolute and relative location of each topic and the amount of space devoted to each'* (p. 1084). Hansen and Haas (1988) offer a framework to explain such findings in terms of the 'page size', 'legibility', 'responsiveness', and 'tangibility' of paper and on-screen texts.

It would be wrong-headed to expect the computer screen's physicality to influence literacy practices consistently across individuals. A supposedly 'given' task may be performed quite differently by different individuals who have their own idiosyncratic ways of accomplishing it. The participants in our screen/paper comparative writing task had previously taken part in a more naturalistic study documenting how they produced a genuine coursework essay. In the genuine coursework situation, they differed quite substantially from each other in how they worked with source materials. In our comparative situation, many of these differences were preserved. Participants constructed different roles for source texts, in line with their established reading practices. What mattered about the materiality of the sources was therefore different for each participant: it depended on the specific roles sources played in their writing practices. For one participant, the technologies 'influenced' performance by facilitating or interfering with *her* established practice of skim-reading and moving frequently between documents. For another participant, the technologies 'influenced' performance by facilitating or interfering with *his* established practice of visiting each document only once and reading it thoroughly from beginning to end. Whether or not the screen 'inhibits' or 'facilitates' a writer's use of text sources, depends heavily on the way any individual, with their own history of practice, performs that task.

Having acknowledged that the influence of the computer screen is contingent upon each individual's shaping of activity, we now suggest the notion that the screen, through its material properties, also itself shapes activity. A number of participants in our study used paper sources quite differently from those presented on screen. They tended to take notes from on-screen documents, and to refer to these notes, not to the texts themselves, when composing. Yet they tended to take no notes from documents available on paper. Rather they highlighted or annotated them, and returned to them throughout writing. Participants typically cited aspects of the materiality of each medium – such as those mentioned above – as reasons for adopting different practices with each medium. Material differences between the two media then, helped shape very different forms of practice and, therefore, different experiences of the texts.

Technology then, can best be understood not as a static influence on literacy practice, but as a dynamic contributor to it. What matters about a technology – the affordances and constraints associated with it – are not properties of the technology *per se*, but emerge only from its relation with the person (and with the rest of the setting) in activity. Furthermore, these affordances and constraints do not simply influence how smoothly or problematically pre-given literacy practices will proceed: they actually shape the practices themselves. Individuals and computers are involved in complex transactions that shape literacy activities.

2. Text on the network

Writing has an inevitable temporal structure. There is a coarsely-grained rhythm that describes when we initiate and terminate separate episodes of engagement with the task. Yet there is also a more fine-grained tempo to writing. This involves a pattern of shifting attention as the writer moves in and out of engagement within a single episode or session. The point of the present section is to highlight how the technological context of the activity serves to choreograph this pattern of involvement. We are particularly concerned here with the more fine-grained level of engagement.

Comments above about manipulating screen-based documents remind us that there is often an issue for writers of coordinating between the writing task itself and a number of supporting resources – such as reference works and other texts. In the previous section, we considered re-mediations of writing that attended to some of the physicality in this coordination of action. Specifically, we illustrated the significance of physicality by developing a contrast involving writers coordinating attention to exclusively screen-based documentary resources. In the present section, we dwell more on the *interactive* dimension of the medium, rather than its spatial qualities. The key issue concerns how the involvement of ICT creates new ways of managing this mobility between resources. Of particular interest is the networked status of the technology in use.

For a writer, the existence of parallel documents ready-to-hand is often important. This is especially true for the case here; namely, the well-researched writing of undergraduates. Typically, students position them-selves to optimize such engagements with support material. By focusing on the networked nature of ICT, we raise issues concerned with computers creating richer possibilities for movement between documents. This is not a point about the sheer quantity of support documents that might be rendered to hand by easy network accessing. Rather it is a point, first, about how ICT reconfigures the whole issue of managing document access. Then, secondly, it is about how ICT necessitates changes in the affordances for interacting with the immediate writing environment. This entails changes in the underlying rhythm of writing – understood as a set of attentional commitments the writer must make to sources. We comment on each of these network features in turn.

To say that ICT entails a reworking of the business of document access raises the issue of how writing gets spread across a variety of different locations. Our diary records from undergraduates indicate that a writing project can be exercised in a wide range of places. Most obviously, in libraries and university resource rooms; but also in common rooms, friends' study bedrooms and, of course, the writer's own living space. To a significant extent, the motive for distributing activity over locations reflects the need to gain access to physical documents that are themselves all over the place. This applies to books and journals but also to material that might need to be borrowed from staff or fellow students.

On the particular campus we studied, private study bedrooms enjoyed intranet and internet access. This meant that some documents that once required trips to teaching spaces (libraries and so on) might now be obtained online in the student's own room. Documents borrowed from fellow students might be routed about the campus via email. Resource room documents have migrated to 'the web'. In short, such networking serves to situate the act of writing more firmly in a single place – the site of one's networked PC. When we compared the diaries of students with network access in their own rooms to those of students without network access we found a number of differences (Crook and Light 2002). We did not find any difference in the absolute amount of private study. However the students with network access were more likely to conduct that study in their private rooms. We assume this applies to their writing assignments – as these represented a large proportion of what private study involved. Campus networking, then, does not precipitate more private study but it reconfigures how that study is done. In particular, it concentrates it more in a single place. Thus the experience of writing becomes more situated in this sense.

This example serves our general purpose. The empirical comparison made possible by partial campus networking allowed us to notice a significant and general feature of student writing as a form of cultural practice. Namely, through an inevitable distribution across sites of social and study activity, writing involves *other people* and, thereby, a potentially wide variety of opportunities for exploration and interaction. ICT (in the form of networked study bedrooms) reconfigures the dynamic of writing practices in that sense. It does so by virtue of its disturbance to the socially-distributed nature of the activity.

The second point we wish to make about networked ICT and writing arises from the strong interactive properties of the networked computer. In this case, we use system logs gathered from a broad sample of students with PCs in their own rooms (Crook and Barrowcliff 2001). The most striking message of these records is that students used this technology a lot. From around mid-day until well into the late evening there was a 50 per cent chance that a study bedroom computer would be active. This hints there are a great many things that can be done with this technology. Indeed, that notion of versatility gets nearer to the main point we wish to make about the finer detail of usage patterns. One distinctive feature of a networked computer is that it makes a large number of resources available at one site for action. Sitting at this technology, the user is able to send electronic mail, have synchronous text conversations, read a news ticker, listen to an MP3 file, watch the television, surf the web – as well as interact with a word processor. All these things may be done in parallel. Perhaps the common image of the PC as a recreational technology is the image of games playing. Yet these students spent rather little time engaged with conventional computer games. Rather, what they did was more about multi-tasking: moving in and out of a wide range of separate applications in a style of working that is best described as 'animated'.

One analysis we conducted concerned all sessions where a word processor was opened for at least an hour and where the document title implied a course-related writing project. System logs allowed the pattern of computer activity across that hour to be followed. On average, during such a word processing session a student would attend to another task (shift input focus) once every four minutes. How this more animated style of writing should be judged is not central to the present discussion. Certainly, some of these movements between computer applications involved movements between resources that were central to the composition task – text files, websites and so forth. However, it was also clear that many such movements serviced more recreational interests – changing background music, responding to instant messages and so on. None of which is to suggest that private spaces have not always been rich in such affordances for fragmenting some core study activity – such as using a word processor for composition. However, ICT creates an additional layer of such alternative possibilities. Writing tasks executed at this networked technology are clearly reconfigured: this is a technology that strikingly concentrates at one site a wide range of highly interactive affordances.

A final point regarding this theme is important, as it echoes something we have already noted about the inherent variation in activities implicating such rich technologies. In interviews it became apparent that students managed the potential of ICT for multi-tasking in different ways. Half of them reported genuine concern that they spent too much time in playful use of their computers. Perhaps as a result of such worries, many reported strategies for filtering out certain sorts of competing computer activities that might be accessible during a period of planned writing. Others, however, seem relaxed about this feature of the technology and were more vigorous in responding to interactive options when they arose. This is the point we have stressed before: individual writers shape the inclusion of new technologies in distinctive ways. Accordingly, simple generalizations about singular 'effects' are again seen to be inappropriate.

3. Text as electronic traffic

This section concerns how writers' involvement with ICT can impart a more fluid quality to their texts. Usually this point would preface a discussion of word processors and the manner in which they allow writers to cut, shape, paste or otherwise manipulate text. Here, however, we consider how text becoming 'fluid' involves manipulations that have a more *social* focus. Early on in the development of computers for education, researchers noticed how this technology could potentially 'socialise the writing process' (Daiute 1983). One way this may be achieved is by recruiting text into practices of interpersonal communication. Evidently, such practices have been cultivated by the popularity of email, instant messaging, chatrooms, and asynchronous discussion forums. Texts composed in such ICT contexts come to acquire distinctive registers (Ferrara, Brunner and Whittemore 1991). However, there are other ways in which computers mediate by entering situations in which learners (or writers) are interacting. That is, computers are a technology for *collaboration*. Joint activity may occur 'at' them, 'around' them and 'through' them (Crook 1994). Accordingly, student writing might become one such species of activity incorporated into any or all those collaborative arrangements.

Undergraduates can be reluctant collaborators in relation to the familiar task of producing essays (Hounsell 1987). Our interviews and diaries suggest that it remains relatively unusual for students to work together 'at' computers in the interests of shared writing. What our interviews do reveal is that student collaboration over study does occur, but with a somewhat improvised or serendipitous quality. This includes unannounced visits to friends' rooms, some developing into work-related exchanges. On such occasions, the desktop computer offers a particularly visible surface for supporting joint composition. It might at the very least precipitate a critical discussion of someone's writing-in-progress. In this sense, the potential for ICT to enter such casual exchanges may implicate the technology in supporting more social forms of writing among students.

However, there is a further sense in which writing is socialized by ICT. This is captured in the idea that computers provide a technology for student peers to interact 'through'. Text can become more fluid by the ease with which it can be passed among computer users populating a common network. Our system logs of networked computers in student study bedrooms revealed that local file transfer via email and instant messaging was very common. Much of the transferred material was not related to the curriculum. Again the computer has emerged as an intriguing technology through the way in which it resources both playful and academic concerns at a single site. Our expectation is that practices of electronic communication that evolve to serve playful interests will be gradually appropriated into study demands. Similarly, undergraduate texts will move more freely among peers thanks to the transporting infrastructure supplied by ICT networking. In this sense literacy will become more social.

What students told us about their shared use of lecture notes reinforced the idea that such trends could be active. Most students reported exchanging notes from lectures. Most students with computers in their private rooms reported doing this via electronic mail. It must be admitted that coursework writing seemed more protected in this sense. Coursework, unlike lectures, was more likely to be a topic of *conversation* – something the student sought benchmarking reassurances about in relation to personal progress. Being more possessive about coursework than lecture notes is perhaps not surprising. Yet some sorts of coursework traffic still should be innocently attractive to students: for instance, passing across material to members of the next class to take the course. In such circumstances it may be lack of everyday contact with this parallel peer cohort that constrains such activity. If so, email may play an increasing role in coursework exchange, as well as lecture note material.

4. Text and the website

The previous section converged on somewhat speculative observations based only upon emerging trends in ICT use. The present section is even more tentative, by virtue of the early development state of relevant ICT structures. Again, the theme is an increasingly social dimension to writing activities. In the previous section, we dwelt upon the potential of ICT for making text more mobile among students, with the expectation that writing would thereby become more socially distributed. It illustrated the sense in which literacy practices are 'social' and the manner in which new technology is involved with this. The concern of the present section is with the role of *audience* in a broader sense. How can ICT be implicated in student literacy through shaping it to become a more public form of intellectual practice?

We now invoke the emerging phenomenon of the academic course website in order to explore notions of audience. University teaching managers increasingly expect academics to make use of web technology to resource students taking their courses. In short, they expect to see course websites. Analysis of what this precipitates in one representative institution (Crook 2002) suggests that academics are not yet very vigorous or imaginative in how they make use of this new infrastructure. Indeed most of them simply do not use it at all. Those that do present fairly pedestrian material dominated by collections of lecture notes. As it happens, this corresponds very closely with what students report they need. Yet, how might it be otherwise?

This was discussed more fully in relation to primary education (Crook 1998). There it was suggested that ICT offered a powerful technology for making visible learner activity within the classroom community. The notion of a course website (or a classroom website) acknowledges the idea that this technology concerns something potentially local in character. Indeed what is found at such sites may well be 'local' in the sense of relating to needs and interests within that learning community. Typically, the origin of such material is the organizer of the course, or the teacher of the class. Here we note that local websites also offer a versatile tool for making visible material that comes from learners themselves. These can be a powerful resource for the traditional challenge of each class to create 'common knowledge' (Edwards and Mercer 1987), and can create an authentic sense of audience among novice writers, as well as resource future generations of learners in a class by virtue of 'leaving tracks'.

The products of much student writing are rarely shared with other people. Often such writing may only be seen by the person who set the task. The sense of genuinely writing for others is important to cultivate; the practices of writing that arise where that motive is in place are likely to be distinctive. Moreover, benefit accrues to 'others' also, through the possibility of vicariously learning from access to the work of peers (Mayes

1995). Outside educational contexts, the web has become a lively forum in which opportunities for creativity in the written word are richly celebrated. Such potential has hardly been explored within universities for the case of student writing. Yet ICT in the form of web-based publishing offers considerable prospects for this further sense of socialized literacy.

The dialogue around text

The previous example conveys again the broad scope of factors we wish to embrace as describing literacy practice for the undergraduate writer. It reminds us of the variety of ways in which the context for producing a text relates to a technical setting. Resources found on a course website are relevant to shaping the form of an undergraduate composition, most controversially (but not inevitably) in terms of offering the student cut-and-paste solutions. However, the course website also has a potential to shape writing activity in another way: through its capacity to create audience. This example serves our purposes in that it allows us to see the way in which literacy practices extend deeply into the socio-cultural context in which the composition is set.

We give now a further example that stresses 'audience' to highlight another dimension of literacy practice liable to re-mediation through new technologies. Most undergraduate writing will have an instrumental quality. It will be constructed to do something. It will be planned to effect some influence on the reader. Most often that reader might be narrowly defined as the person who sets the task or, more generally, the person who grades the work. In short, much student writing gets positioned in a loop of feedback. It forms the basis of a possible dialogue between student and tutor. This feedback contract overarches the production of any particular piece of writing. It characterizes part of the general cultural setting in which the undergraduate writes. As such it must be a pervasive influence on the writing enterprise.

We believe that the dialogue cultivated by a piece of written work is an interesting but neglected dimension of a student's developing literacy practice. Also, the form of that dialogue is significantly coloured by the nature of specialized technical and social practices that are used to manage it. Traditionally, such tutorial feedback on writing was a strongly inter-personal event. At its most elaborate, it might involve a student in some detailed one-to-one discussion with a tutor, focused on some com-position that the student had submitted. More recently, such feedback may have been distilled into something a little more terse: corrections noted on the text, comments made in margins, evaluative remarks appended to the finished product. While more economical in form, these practices arguably still maintain a strong flavour of an interpersonal exchange prompted by the student composition.

Such scribbles, notes and evaluative remarks can be viewed as the 'social practice' underpinning this particular form of tutorial dialogue. Accordingly, we can imagine instruments – alternative forms of mediation – that could be inserted into this process, and which might alter it in significant ways. The example presented in Figure 6.1 is a case in point. It is a form of technology for managing the feedback obligation: namely, a coursework coversheet through which tutor comments can be organized and attached to the work in question. Interestingly, its design critically depends upon the availability of ICT. Printing assignment-specific details to cover the many courses taught in a large university department requires the computational help of a teaching programme database. What is made possible by that technology is a single sheet of paper that summarizes the teaching context for each assignment; included in its design is space for a tutor to mark and comment on the work itself. The example in Figure 6.1 is based on a real case in active use, although details identifying the department have been edited.

The instrument was originally conceived to be only in the best interests of good teaching and learning practice. It is not for us to judge whether it has been successful in that sense: not least, because we have no empirical evidence that is directly relevant to the question. However, the example remains a good basis for general consideration of this aspect of students' literacy practices. What the instrument achieves is a method for proceduralizing the act of feedback. Probably, the stimulus for doing so was a well-intentioned one based upon the ambition to ensure that a minimal level of tutor commentary did occur. Yet there is a danger that such proceduralization renders the feedback less personal, perhaps serving to create a sense that a social exchange has been reified (Wenger 1998).

It would be useful to understand how the feedback impact is altered by practices that seem to mechanize the communication involved. Even the more modest tradition of marginal scribbles and summary comments at the end of a composition conveys a sense of managing an authentic dialogue with the reader. That sense of student writing being a literacy practice includes an embedding of text in an institutional conversation. ICT can act to re-mediate the form of that exchange

Concluding remarks

Perhaps understanding the significance of ICT in psychological domains can be impeded by the bounded nature of this technology. For this technology seems conveniently self-contained as a material tool. Accordingly, experimentally-minded researchers may be drawn to isolate design features of the tool, features that may be explored as independent variables in experiments. It is certainly easy to tinker in this spirit with

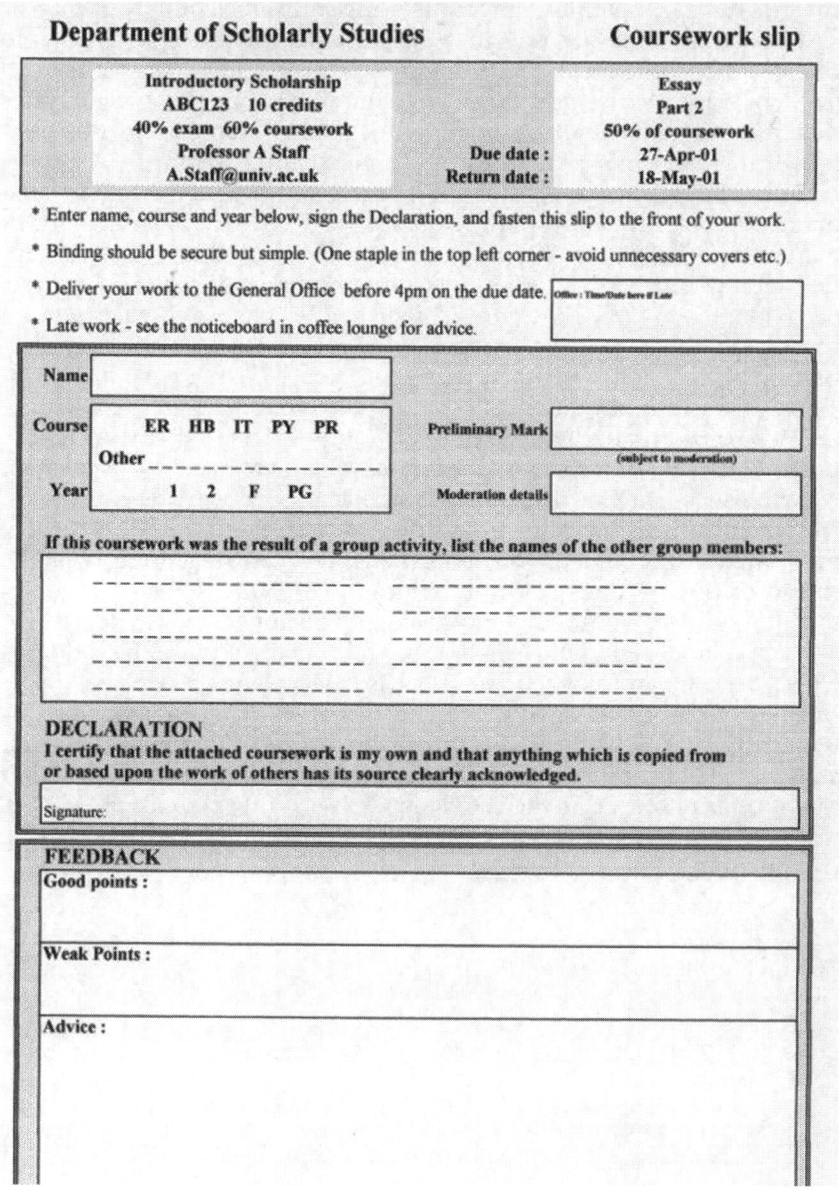

Department of Scholarly Studies   **Coursework slip**

Introductory Scholarship ABC123 10 credits 40% exam 60% coursework Professor A Staff A.Staff@univ.ac.uk	Due date : Return date :	Essay Part 2 50% of coursework 27-Apr-01 18-May-01

* Enter name, course and year below, sign the Declaration, and fasten this slip to the front of your work.

* Binding should be secure but simple. (One staple in the top left corner - avoid unnecessary covers etc.)

* Deliver your work to the General Office before 4pm on the due date. `Office : Time/Date here if Late`

* Late work - see the noticeboard in coffee lounge for advice.

Name

Course   ER   HB   IT   PY   PR   Preliminary Mark

Other _ _ _ _ _ _ _ _ _ _ _ _ _ _ _ _ _ _   (subject to moderation)

Year   1   2   F   PG   Moderation details

If this coursework was the result of a group activity, list the names of the other group members:

_ _ _ _ _ _ _ _ _ _ _ _ _ _ _ _ _ _   _ _ _ _ _ _ _ _ _ _ _ _ _ _ _ _ _ _
_ _ _ _ _ _ _ _ _ _ _ _ _ _ _ _ _ _   _ _ _ _ _ _ _ _ _ _ _ _ _ _ _ _ _ _
_ _ _ _ _ _ _ _ _ _ _ _ _ _ _ _ _ _   _ _ _ _ _ _ _ _ _ _ _ _ _ _ _ _ _ _
_ _ _ _ _ _ _ _ _ _ _ _ _ _ _ _ _ _   _ _ _ _ _ _ _ _ _ _ _ _ _ _ _ _ _ _
_ _ _ _ _ _ _ _ _ _ _ _ _ _ _ _ _ _   _ _ _ _ _ _ _ _ _ _ _ _ _ _ _ _ _ _

DECLARATION
I certify that the attached coursework is my own and that anything which is copied from
or based upon the work of others has its source clearly acknowledged.

Signature:

FEEDBACK
Good points :

Weak Points :

Advice :

Figure 6.1   An anonymized coversheet generated by a computer database to service the commentary made by tutors on student writing

the functional properties of text processing software. Similarly, it may be easy to tinker with the way in which this ICT object is inserted into the teaching contexts. Approaching ICT as a convenient cluster of independent variables is only possible if researchers are also comfortable that there is some similarly bounded dependent variable: in this case, something that can be straightfowardly measured as 'writing'.

Historically, it has proved tempting to regard writing as activity that does have this singular (and measurable) quality. The core activity of manipulating a pen or keyboard seems to give it this focus. Perhaps no writing researcher frames their interest in quite such a narrow behavioural way. Yet the sense in which researchers approach writing more as 'literacy practice' often takes us no further than another relatively narrow behavioural repertoire: that associated with the construction of plans, drafts and annotations. We have argued that the practice of writing involves more than these traditional points of research focus. In the present chapter, we have chosen examples that help make visible a much wider sense in which writing must be studied.

Hopefully, it is evident from these examples that ICT is deeply implicated in the undergraduate's experience of writing. So rapid is the spread of this technology within educational contexts that it becomes urgent to understand the significance of its role for student writers. However, that understanding can not be grounded in research traditions wherein claims are made about how isolated technical variables have singular effects on isolated dependent variables. The influence in this ICT-writing relationship is very much one of reconfiguring. The availability of ICT is ensuring that writing gets done differently. Our ability to notice just how it is re-mediated requires us to use methods of observation and analysis that respect the systemic nature of this ICT/writing conjunction.

References

Bruce, B.C. (1997) Literacy technologies: what stance should we take? *Journal of Literacy Research*, 29: 289–309.

Cole, M. (1996) *Cultural Psychology*. Cambridge: Cambridge University Press.

Cole, M. and Griffen, P. (1980) Cultural amplifiers reconsidered, in D.R. Olson (ed.) *The Social Foundations of Language and Thought*. New York: Norton.

Crook, C.K. (1994) *Computers and the Collaborative Experience of Learning*. London: Routledge.

Crook, C.K. (1998) Computers in the community of classrooms, in K. Littleton and P. Light (eds) *Learning with Computers: Analysing Productive Interaction*. London: Routledge.

Crook, C.K. (in press) The campus experience of networked learning, in C. Steeples and C. Jones (eds) *Networked Learning*. Berlin: Springer-Verlag.

Crook, C.K. and Barrowcliff, D. (2001) Ubiquitous computing on campus: patterns of engagement by university students, *International Journal of Human Computer Interaction*, 13: 245–58.

Crook, C.K. and Light, P.H. (in press) Virtual society and the cultural practice of learning, in S. Woolgar (ed.) *Virtual Society?* Oxford: Oxford University Press.

Daiute, C. (1985) Issues in using computers to socialize the writing process, *Educational Computing and Technology Journal*, 33: 41–50.

Dillon, A. (1992) Reading from paper versus screens – a critical-review of the empirical literature, *Ergonomics*, 35: 1297–326.

Dymott, R. and Crook, C.K. (2001a) Ethnographic analysis of student essay production: technology mediated practices. Paper presented to 8th Annual Conference of Writing Development in Higher Education: Changing Contexts for Teaching and Learning, Leicester, 24–25 April.

Dymott, R. and Crook, C.K. (2001b) Student essay production: more than a problem solving task. Paper presented at International Conference on Communication, Problem Solving and Learning, Glasgow, Scotland, 25–29 June.

Edwards, D. and Mercer, N. (1987) *Common Knowledge*. London: Methuen.

Erickson, B.J. (1992) A synthesis of studies on computer-supported composition, revision, and quality, *Journal of Research on Computing in Education*, 25: 172–86.

Ferrara, K., Brunner, H. and Whittemore, G. (1991) Interactive written discourse as an emergent register, *Written Communication*, 8: 8–34.

Hansen, W.J. and Haas, C. (1988) Reading and writing with computers: a framework for explaining differences in performance, *Communications of the ACM*, 31: 1080–9.

Hayes, J. and Flower, L. (1980) Identifying the organization of writing processes, in R. Gregg and R. Steinberg (eds) *Cognitive Processes in Writing*. Hillsdale, NJ: LEA.

Hounsell, D. (1987) Essay writing and the quality of feedback, in J. Richardson, M. Eysenck and D. Piper (eds) *Student Learning: Research in Education and Cognitive Psychology*. Milton Keynes: SRHE and Open University Press.

Hutchins, E.L., Hollan, J.D. and Norman, D.A. (1986) Direct manipulation interfaces, in D. Norman and S. Draper (eds) *User-Centered System Design*. Hillsdale, N.J.: Lawrence Erlbaum.

Kellogg, R.T. and Mueller, S. (1993) Performance amplification and process restructuring in computer based writing, *International Journal of Man-Machine Studies*, 39: 33–49.

Mayes, J.T. (1995) Learning technology and groundhog day, in W. Strang, V. Simpson and D. Slater (eds) *Hypermedia at Work: Practice and Theory in Higher Education*. Canterbury: University of Kent Press.

O'Hara, K. and Sellen, A. (1997) A comparison of reading paper and online documents, *Proceedings of CHI '97*, 22–27 March.

Ransdell, S.E. and Levy, C.M. (1994) Writing as process and product – the impact of tool, genre, audience knowledge, and writer expertise, *Computers in Human Behavior*, 10: 511–27.

Snyder, I. (1993) Writing with word processors: a research overview, *Review of Educational Research*, 35: 49–65.

Torrance, M. (1996) Is writing expertise like other kinds of expertise? in G. Rijlaarsdam, H. van den Bergh and M. Couzin (eds) *Theories, Models and Methodology in Writing Research*. Amsterdam: Amsterdam University Press.

Wenger, E. (1998) *Communities of Practice*. Cambridge: Cambridge University Press.

7

'MY SON'S NEVER OPENED A BOOK, BUT I CAN'T GET HIM OFF THE COMPUTER': TEENAGE DISCOURSE AND COMPUTER GAMES

Noel Williams

Introduction

In this chapter I want to discuss some of the key characteristics of the new literacies. My title comes from a conversation I overheard in a bus queue. I argue that the worry represented by this popular complaint may well be unnecessary. Whilst some people may see conflict between traditional notions of print-based literacy and the new ICT literacy, this need not be the case. I illustrate the complex relationship between these two views of literacy by considering a case study of a group of adolescent computer game players. I argue that in many ways the versions of literacy adolescents can learn from the culture of computer games is more useful and relevant to the digital world than the versions they may acquire in the classroom.

First, I consider what might be meant by 'literacy' in this context, as establishing the communicative value of any computer-based discourse depends very much on the richness of the concept of literacy being used. Then I suggest that the computer game itself may be regarded as a communicative artefact about which we may be more, or less, literate, before exploring the communicative practices of computer games' players. I sketch several different branches of games playing which all seem to require, develop and perhaps enhance communicative abilities. This review of games players' communications allows me to conclude that computer games may at least develop some adolescents' language skills, but also, more radically, that perhaps educational concepts of literacy need adaptation to better reflect digital practice as evidenced by the adept adolescent.

Literacy or literacies?

The advent of ICTs has undercut traditional notions of literacy. In Catherine Beavis' words: 'the need for literacy to be reconceptualised and redefined in the face of rapid change seems overwhelming' (Beavis 1999). If we survey contemporary literature on literacy, we find discussion not of *literacy*, but of *literacies*. Each discipline, it seems, if it has any concern with human communication, is offering its own analysis of the way forward in the move from print-based to computer-based literacy.

Each characterizes literacy and the consequent role of ICTs differently. 'Media literacy' concerns understanding and reproduction of media-based messages, sees ICTs as mass media, and users of ICTs as producers and reproducers of cultural messages. (See, for example, Silverblatt 2000). Compare 'Publishing literacy' which is the 'the ability to format and publish research and ideas electronically, in textual and multimedia forms (including via World Wide Web, electronic mail and distribution lists, and CD-ROMs), to introduce them into the electronic public realm and the electronic community of scholars' (Shapiro and Hughes 1996). Here the focus is on ICT users as *disseminators* not consumers or producers. Publishing literacy is presented as one element of 'information literacy' (Ibid.). Information literacy derives from the discipline of information science, within which ICTs are a subset of archival systems and delivery mechanisms for ideas and information.

Compare this with 'Information design' whose focus is authors and designers. They see ICTs as fundamental in their professional contexts (offering tools for the integration and better construction of complex messages) but also as requiring the new skills of those who create public information, integrating the textual, graphical and computational. Their concern is with 'design literacy', 'multimedia literacy' and 'visual literacy'. This in turn is taken up by semioticians and cultural theorists who note a shift from the verbal to the visual in contemporary texts, and a consequent shift in the nature of reading:

Whereas the old-fashioned book was read from beginning to end, this new book is not read at all, it is used. The shift here has been from an older organisation of text to a newer organisation of resource; from an

NOEL WILLIAMS

older concern with knowledge to a newer concern with gathering information to manage a task demanded by, or set, in a unit of work.
(Kress 1997)

What this volatile and somewhat fuzzy literature represents on the one hand is the interplay of many disciplines as they seek to come to terms with the new technology, and compete for the right to determine its theoretical base. On the other hand, it represents the inherent complexity of trying to establish such a theoretical base, for the new literacies are not merely concerned with reading and writing. Words may be at their heart, but they also require understanding, in some sense, of information science, of social context, of oracy, of multiple media, of design and publication, of digital coding and of graphic design. Literacy has not been a constant but an evolving concept, and, as Mark Warschauer suggests: ICTs are simply making educators review their concepts of literacy more rapidly than in any previous era (Warschauer 1999).

The consensus seems to be that literacy can no longer be viewed as a set of content neutral, transferable skills, but as a sociocultural phenomenon, communicative practices embedded in particular social and cultural contexts (see, for example, Warschauer 1997). Traditional rhetoric emphasized the purpose of the speech or writing. Today mainstream teaching of writing emphasizes purpose and audience, and focuses on writing as a process. Reading is seen increasingly as an intertextual phenomenon; understanding of one text can depend critically on familiarity with others. Contemporary literacy, communication through ICTs requires all this contextual understanding, but a great deal more besides. Effective communication may more than ever depend on accurate understanding of, and manipulation of, the context. Moreover this understanding and use requires a wider range of skills, and increasing flexibility in their application.

The new type of writing/authoring skills required include the following:

1) Being able to integrate texts, graphics, and audio-visual material into multimedia presentations
2) Being able to write effectively in hypertext genres
3) Being able to deploy internal and external links to communicate a message well
4) Being able to write for a particular audience when the audience is unknown readers on the World Wide Web
5) Using effective pragmatic strategies in various circumstances of computer-mediated communication, including one-to-one email, email discussion lists, and real-time online discussion.
(Warschauer 1999b)

As an author employing new communications, this list covers perhaps the minimum of required skills, for this list of Warschauer's is focused on the task of *producing* messages. In addition, however, the user of ICTs must be a reader of such messages, and to be a reader, she must also be a finder and evaluator of what she finds. These skills might be characterized as traditional skills of information search (as employed in a print library) and summary. However, ICTs demand not merely an enhancement of such skills, but the ability to engage in *qualitatively* different processes. The internet, being a representation of a social information network, demands not merely information retrieval skills, but also (to use it well) social communicative skills, to discover appropriate materials effectively, to evaluate them efficiently and to integrate them in ways that unknown users ('readers') may find acceptable. The shift from document as knowledge to document as resource (in Kress' terms) means that the ICT user has to construct knowledge for her or himself out of the dialogic with the whole available resource.

These are the skills characterized by Paul Gilster as 'digital literacy', and it is perhaps this looser term, defined by the medium not by the content or use of that medium which is most useful in encapsulating the knowledge modern learners need (Gilster 1997). Gilster provides an excellent review of the information skills required for effective and efficient use of the internet, and argues that each of those skills requires a particular sensitivity specific to the computer-networked context. Using a search engine is not using a catalogue. Searching the web is not searching for book titles. Judging available information cannot be independent of the quality of the search employed. And so on. Reading on the internet is not merely a process of understanding, but of constant evaluation: judging the quality of what is received, selecting from multiple disparate offerings, assessing when to choose a hypertext link and deviate from the linear norm. Writing for the internet is not merely about assembling information and constructing appropriate expression of that information. It requires understanding of the different needs of different audiences, a sense of their ephemeral contact with your information, an ability to distil the key content, and skills in for-mulating words appropriate to the medium and context. Certainly we would judge that such skills are desirable at the higher levels of literacy in print cultures. But in using ICTs for communication, they are essential.

In this context, one new communicative form which may encourage, even enable, learners to develop appropriate abilities, is the computer game. Recently, some researchers have begun to consider the computer game as a communicative form in itself, and to wonder if there may be properties of employing such media which are of intrinsic educational benefit (see, for example, the work of Catherine Beavis, who believes that games with a narrative component may be examined with the same literary purposes as print literature. Beavis 1998 and Beavis 1999). Beavis suggests that computer games may be studied in the same framework as conventional literature in the classroom, albeit in her work still in the context of educational research:

> We took a deliberately literary approach to the non-literary game to underline the workings of the text as narrative and to highlight continuities between games and other forms – novel and film primarily – in the construction and reading/playing of the game. Students were asked to think of themselves as readers, and the game as story, in their discussion and writing about the game.
>
> (Beavis 1999)

As Paul Gilster (1997) argues: 'Literacy in the digital age – digital literacy – is partly about awareness of other people and our expanded ability to contact them to discuss issues and get help. But it is also an awareness of the way the internet blends older forms of communication to create a different kind of content.' Digital literacy is at once about the social networks technologies facilitate, and digital convergence, the rapid integration of different media and different forms of communication. The computer game is a key example of both, being both a key to (some) adolescent discourse and a discourse itself formed from converging media. Digital literacy may be facilitated both in and through computer games.

Computer games and literacy

The stereotype of the adolescent computer gamer is the lone teenager, isolated in his room (and it generally is a 'him'), hunched over the keyboard uncommunicatively in pursuit of simulated death and destruction. This stereotypical nerd is so consumed with the game that he rejects social interaction, so enrapt in interacting with the screen that he has no time to open a book, and so self-absorbed that he never picks up a pen. In this view the computer game is demonized and the teenage player is seen as antisocial, uncommunicative and illiterate, an unlearning slave to the keyboard.

In many ways this popular image seems fundamentally to misrepresent the subculture of modern computer games, and perhaps to miss completely the communicative forms which teenage players engage in as part of their subculture. I want to explore the hypothesis that, far from removing teenagers from communicative situations and restricting their opportunities for language use, modern games almost necessarily involve players in a communicative network where new verbal skills are required and existing ones developed.

At one level we can be reasonably clear about what we would like adolescents to achieve in their knowledge and use of computers. This is the level where knowledge is application specific. Teaching a child how to use Windows or Word or Explorer is a clearly defined task where outcomes can be defined and achievement measured.

A more abstract level of ability, above that of specific knowledge of specific applications, is harder to be firm about: being 'digitally literate' may mean knowing about operating systems or text editors or databases, rather than the specific skills associated with a specific application. Yet we can still stipulate with a degree of clarity the kind of expertise we would expect to be able to see. Being able to use and understand databases is more than simply being able to cut and paste in Access, but competent use of Access is one indicator of that understanding.

However, there is a level of conceptualization above this in which 'digital literacy' means a flexible understanding of the whole fluid medium, enabling informed and appropriate choice and use of all the functionality associated with that medium. This level of literacy is not merely application independent, but system independent. It is knowledge of how to achieve a communicative purpose given available ICTs, irrespective of what the particular ICT or purpose is, to use it efficiently, effectively and creatively. It demands widespread knowledge of available functions, the ability to make complex choices between them, skills in critical evaluation of competing media and messages, and the ability to assemble well-chosen appropriate messages in both very open and very constrained contexts.

With rapid increases in the pervasiveness and the approachability of modern interfaces, knowledge at the application specific level, where much educational effort is focused, seems less and less appropriate. Educationalists perhaps need to worry less about delivering the specifics of a given computer technology and less about the impact of the dynamically evolving medium on traditional book-based concepts of literacy, and focus more on the literate concepts and skills which adolescents may acquire, employ or require in their actual use of ICTs, beyond merely their impact on the norms of communication implied by the focus on book-based learning. To put this more starkly, does favouring a computer over a book imply a loss of literacy, or more a transformation to a different norm for 'the literate'? Is it possible that a strong focus on print culture may interfere with the acquisition of more relevant and meaningful digital skills?

So a proper exploration of teenage literacy needs to examine the extent to which ICT skills may:

a) dilute or distract from traditional concepts of forms of literacy;
b) transfer to those traditional skills of literacy and oracy;
c) transform those skills into something new, a new set of competences, which are perhaps being learned without being taught.

If adolescents spend large parts of their leisure time playing computer games, surfing the web or interacting in chatrooms are we to be concerned because we see this activity as essentially (a)? Or should we be seeking to identify those communicative values present in such systems which we can map onto the traditional, preferred educational practice, using the ever-present machine to benefit (b)? Or should we rather be shifting educational practice to reflect and promote precisely the communication practices these recent media require, and move the curriculum and even pedagogy towards (c)?

In the rest of this chapter I am going to work from the assumption that (a) is largely a reactionary error. I want to explore the literacies adolescent gamers actually require and acquire.

The discourses of computer games

To pursue some of these ideas I engaged in a microstudy of a small group of adolescent computer gamers, to explore their actual practice and the ways in which they constructed discourse around their activity. Are each of these gamers isolated nerds immured in antisocial electronic uncommunicativity? Or are they highly communicative, sociable experts, exploring and developing language as they dip into their electronic box of delights?

You can see, of course, from the way I phrase this, that my observations suggest more of the latter than the former. This small group is made up of my two sons and their coterie, six adolescent males in total. Each is something of a gaming fanatic, though their gaming extends beyond computers. Each, considered separately, bears some of the stereotypical stigma of the nerd: reluctance to abandon the machine; a disinclination to major physical activity; game play of several hours at a time; interest in the latest tech, the latest releases, the next enhancement; immersion in a popular culture of fantasy and simulated conflict expressed through many media (action films, collectable card games (CCGs), comic books, tabletop wargames, computer games).

There was no tight method about my approach. It was entirely exploratory. I observed the group, and individuals, playing games. I obtained transcripts of their chat, and of other chatrooms they frequented. I taped some of their conversation about games, and I asked them questions on areas that interested me. The entire study was driven by a desire simply to see what sort of discourse(s) they engaged in, in their natural day-to-day play, looking in particular for instances of novel, self-referential or complex language use.

As a group these six are not an aggregation of individuals. They have a social dynamic around the machine, a developing language, and a complex web of communication which is substantially, though not entirely, machine-mediated. Like any specialist group, they have their own jargon, and induction into the group is very much induction into the language of computer gaming as well as the practice. There is no doubt that they are very literate in their medium: they command a wide and flexible vocabulary, they recognize and mobilize complex concepts such as those of genre and form, using critical strategies in many ways similar to those of literary review and classic rhetorical strategy, they have effective and efficient real-time codes that enable them to communicate about a game as they engage in it.

Gaming activities are often one-player on one machine, but are also often flexible social events – a friend comes round, and they play a game as a dyad, perhaps sharing gameplay but also sharing game experience, where one will sit at the shoulder of the other and they will comment on behaviour, activity, ability, affective states, the nature of the interaction, the quality of the experience, they will offer hints and hindsight, make suggestions for strategies, share similar experiences, console and applaud. Or they may gather as a group, with some playing whilst others indulge in some other activity, or with a rotating movement from machine to machine, game to game, player to player, sharing their experiences as a collective. The experienced player will advise and induct the novice to a particular game. The group will share expertise in deciding the best of competing games when new purchases are in order.

Similar observations are reported by other researchers, such as Beavis (1999):

Contrary to popular images, playing games in this situation was intensely social and interactive, with three to four students grouped around a single screen, working the controls, reading the instructions, taking notes of what appeared on screens, trying out solutions, arguing and so on.

When physically separate these players still maintain their social discourse around their games. They may phone or email each other for help or solutions, or to offer information on new systems. These contacts may be entirely about games, or embedded in other cultural discourse (TV, cinema, school, clubbing). They will only choose between email, IRC, mobile phone or landline on practical grounds (e.g. which one is readily available) and seem to make no distinction of purpose between the different media: a given communicative purpose may be delivered through any of these media, and therefore may be spoken or written, synchronous or asynchronous.

This suggests therefore that, at this level of communication, there is no distinction to be made between their literate, oral or computer skills – choosing and using the medium is almost entirely a matter of convenience, and writing, talking and computing are seen as neutral in terms of the demands made upon the communicator. Furthermore, there is clearly a very real sense in which this group of gamers at least maintains a lively social group through and around computer gaming: their games are a keen source of interaction, and a rich stimulus to communication.

However, the quality and nature of that communication perhaps is limited. Are they not operating in a restricted world, their horizons defined ultimately by the commercial concerns of Microsoft, Sony and Lucasarts? Is not their vocabulary a construct of gaming magazines, and their creativity circumscribed by a few mouse movements and keypresses? What language do they use?

Creativity

Arguably internet chat stimulates users to a creative manipulation of language which they would not otherwise engage in. Creativity often results where restrictions of a medium have to be overcome to enable the desired communication. At the level of informativeness internet relay chat (IRC) may carry little of great educational value. But at the level of inventiveness, it may liberate learners who find conventional or traditional communicative modes artificial, irrelevant or unsatisfying.

Christopher Werry's study of IRC, though it did not focus on adolescents specifically, noted that:

> Throughout the textual dialogues that occur on IRC, one can identify a common impulse: an almost manic tendency to produce auditory and visual effects in writing . . . one is reminded of the efforts various writers in the eighteenth century made to produce written language that captured the 'music' of speech, its distinctive tones, timbres and patterns of intonation . . . Interlocutors frequently construct graphic simulations of sounds such as laughter, exclamations, snarls, barks, singing, the sound of racing cars, and various other noises . . . One can discern an intensified engagement with the sounds of language, with the auditory and iconographic potential of words.
>
> (Werry 1996: 58–9)

I found exactly the same creative impulse in the transcripts of adolescent game chat. It would take an extensive and formal study to categorize the creative activities of game chatrooms with some certainty and completeness, but in the examples I looked at, I found:

Creative use of language	Specific device	Examples
Creativity in names	Playful, ironic or attributive eponyms	iceology Oh_look_a_Decoy Blue-Screen-of-Death Fatman
	Graphological or phonological form	KrAyZiE_BoNe Wolfpacx Love2Play
Representation of voice	Scottish accent	look at hees heed its lake an arounge oon a toohpack
	Shouting	HELLO!
Patterning and repetition	Manic laugh	ahahahahahaaa!!
	Protracted intonation, e.g. scream or emphasis	'that's soo much', 'noooooo', 'aaaawwwww'
Phonetic or 'aural' abbreviation	Use of letter sounds	'sux' 'plz' for 'please'
	Use of letter names	'lo' for 'hello' 'cya' for 'see ya'
	Abbreviation	'prolly' for 'probably'

Clearly in such examples, these adolescent lads are playing with language in unrestrained ways with a richness well beyond what they are likely to produce when asked, for example, to write a poem in class. They are searching for effects, stretching the medium, exploring both the constraints and the liberation of the medium, and revelling in it.

As an example of pushing the medium, consider the use of 'smileys' or 'emoticons', which is rampant both online and in text-messaging. Smileys are combinations of punctuation marks used in a loosely iconic way. But they are used not merely to label an attitude or emotional slant which words are inappropriate for – they are now a creative medium themselves. In a minor way, this is a new, and still developing, form of communication.

There are websites which simply act as repositories for smileys, a new communicative resource. Whilst such lists are as much a sign of a desire to be creative with sideways punctuation marks as a wish to communicate nuances of meaning that plain text has difficulty with (the origin of the emoticon or smiley), they also offer a new tool for creative communication. Users may strive to create new, interesting, challenging images through punctuation including, of course, following the creative impulses of obscene graffiti. Examples such as ':-F' (a buck-tooth vampire with one tooth missing) or 'C=}>;*{))' (A drunk, devilish chef, with a toupee in an updraft, moustache, and double chin) can have no other explanation.

These elaborate artefacts are the result of collaborative creativity – as one communicator adds a new twist, the next user twists it further. Whether literacy of this kind counts for much in equipping a games player for the wider world of communication is questionable. But this play is endemic to the medium, and extends into the face-to-face talk of the gaming group. When I asked my group of games players to explain some of the strange verbal devices they used online, the explanation I was given was 'it's how we talk', and there are certainly some correspondences between the flip language of internet chat and the in-group buzz of face-to-face adolescent chatter.

So this creativity is not limited to the computer medium. There was strong evidence in my group that the devices developed in their internet game chat are transferred back into their face-to-face communication. They will, for example, commonly abbreviate the titles of games to their initial letters, as any jargon-rid specialist group may do.

Some of this transference from net to face-to-face is perhaps a little self-conscious, like much else of the self-focused dialogue of adolescent in-group conversation. It perhaps represents not only their interests, but also a tacit mutual confirmation of their perceived sophistication. For example, they will use 'lol' as a meta-comment within real talk for 'that's funny' (i.e. 'laugh out loud'). Common use, however, is probably a little more sophisticated, as it probably indicates irony (i.e. 'that's not really funny, but it's meant to be'). 'Lol' is now a word in their vocabulary, an acronym for an ironic pose.

Error or empowerment?

It would not be too difficult to see adolescent email and online chat as error-ridden symptoms of a casual attitude to text and literate values. Many of the conventions associated with formal writing are abandoned or at least frequently violated in such communication. Spelling, orthography, grammar and punctuation are all ignored (for the sake of simplicity and speed) or manipulated (for effect, to convey special meanings, to speed communication or sometimes, it seems, simply for fun). Many of these features are driven by the constraints of system and situation. Much online language use bears many features that are a function of the medium. (See, for example, Moran and Hawisher 1997 for a review.) As Collot and Belmore have suggested, this medium requires that features both of writing and speech are incorporated (Collot and Belmore 1996).

Yet some studies of learners using online communications seem to suggest that they can result in improved language use. Warschauer (working with adult ESL learners) noted that 'the electronic discussions involved significantly more complex language than the face-to-face discussions' (Warschauer 1996). Lea suggests that learners use online debate to develop stronger rhetorical strategies which transfer to their writing practice, though this is where the online debate is also focused on the writing task (Lea 2000). It seems at least plausible that the richness of the interaction in online chat is likely to stimulate creativity in learners, make them more aware of language and more able to adapt its resources to their needs.

Perhaps these adolescent users are doing no more than removing inherent redundancy in the language in order to strip it down to something more useful and universal. Arguably there is a tension here between the demands of traditional literacy, that writers conform to the communicative conventions endemic in permanent communication (writing) and the ephemeral nature of the task and its throwaway verbal support. There is, for example, little need to signal the start of a sentence through capitalization, if the typical length of any utterance is only one sentence, which is the case for most utterances in internet chat. Why punctuate when the extra key presses merely add redundancy to self-evident statements?

But this assessment is itself oversimplified. Internet chat communication is not merely a case of abandoning all constraints in order to speed up communication. Users on many occasions seem to take *more* time in carrying out operations which are superfluous to the informational needs of the utterance. At times it is almost as if the language has been pared down to a core set of devices in order to embellish it with new effects or meanings, effects which entertain the users and meanings which satisfy in ways beyond that of self-centred gaming. Much of the amusement generated through such codes comes from manipulating the newly honed flexible language, and much of the pleasure is that derived from sharing meaning with others, with communicating something different, unusual, or special.

For example, one set of threads I recorded in gameroom chat gradually evolved, and then abandoned, experiment with spurious URLs as a form of communication:

<Xevius>	www.zipit.com.org
<Drx>	cool
<Drx>	www.whystopilikeurls.com
<[UKF]Mean_Machine>	www.dontbesad.com
<Xevius>	www.stopsendinglinks.com
<Prozac{1}>	lol
<[PAC]Deathbent[GAM]>	www.shutup.com
<BREAKDOWN>	wazzzzaaaaapppp
<Drx>	www.why.com
<Punisher_C__>	www.cs.com
<Xevius>	write to You@here.net
<Drx>	www.hi_breakdown.com
<[PAC]Deathbent[GAM]>	enough with the links already

```
<Prozac{1}>              www.imgonnawhipyourass.com
<Xevius>                 gopher.shutup.com
<Drx>                    i_will_kill_you@ten_oclock.ok?
<Prozac{1}>              www.gayspye.com
                                     (Verbatim chat: Gamespy 1996)
```

Why do this? If the aim is to communicate as quickly and as simply as possible, what is the point of holding an entire conversation in the form of URLs, with superfluous characters and unnecessary punctuation? Clearly this is fun. But not only is it fun, it is an opportunity for some of the communicators at least to experiment with this temporarily discovered form and, in doing so, to show a degree of wit, as in the spurious address 'i_will_kill_you@ten_oclock.ok?', with its simultaneous use of two different syntaxes. As with the use of smileys, the new medium induces some gamers to play with its intrinsic features, and potentially to develop it further.

Nor do these adolescents violate the conventions uncritically. There are numerous instances of users calling attention to their own language or that of others, though this seems more evident in discussion groups than in chat. I have a file from a listserv discussion group on wargames which includes in three months on this discussion eight separate threads on grammar and spelling. Users may send out requests for particular vocabulary, may comment on perceived oddities or errors or unusual usage in others' communication, or may request clarification of wording.

For some users at least it may be that the use of this medium foregrounds such conventions, and leads some communicators to debate such items where they might otherwise remain uncontested. From an educational perspective, there is a clear indication here that using the medium foregrounds the act of communication, and therefore the features it demands of its users can themselves be focused on as legitimate items of learning.

Text structures and genres

Computer games, being themselves texts may induce in players some discursive knowledge beyond that required merely to communicate through computers. Communicating about computer games in part, at least, seems to require specialist textual expertise. This requires a knowledge of genres and their features, and a language for comparative analysis of those genres, and, given the narrative component of many such games, it may also require the vocabulary and conceptualization of narrative.

It is not hard to find examples of comparison and analysis of games which mobilize such vocabulary, though sometimes the discussion is thin:

\<ThaGraveDigga\>	ur saying theres a better single 3d shooter than half life?
\<Loki\>	yes
\<ThaGraveDigga\>	single player?
\<Loki\>	by far – more levels – wepons – items
\<ThaGraveDigga\>	every played system shock?
\<Loki\>	smarter AI
\<Loki\>	no
\<ThaGraveDigga\>	oh
\<Loki\>	ive hear it sucked
\<ThaGraveDigga\>	system shock 2 is suppose to be the one of the best 3d comp shooters
\<ThaGraveDigga\>	its newer
\<Loki\>	how many wepons are in half life
\<Loki\>	cool
\<ThaGraveDigga\>	HL is 2 years old remember heh (TEXT OMITTED)
\<Loki\>	but if it was just single player it would be only ok
\<Loki\>	not great
\<ThaGraveDigga\>	i though sp was good man
\<ThaGraveDigga\>	lots of surprises and stuff
\<Loki\>	the online gameing is what make it
\<Druidity\>	dont 4get the mods . . .

(Verbatim chat from 'Gamespy Arcade': Gamespy 1996)

Clearly this is not sophisticated critical exegesis. Nevertheless it uses a critical and evaluative vocabulary, it makes comparisons between different examples of a genre, attempting to achieve a quite sensitive positioning in a perceived hierarchy, it employs the specialist jargon of the afficianado, it considers different elements which might be put forward as criteria for judgement (number of levels and weapons, the intelligence of the system, the age of the system, the nature of play, and the modifications, by which is meant the additional versions of the game created by players). We even have a hint that the narrative of play is considered by one player as an evaluative criterion ('lots of surprises and stuff').

Narrative structure is one component of gameplay, a major factor in player satisfaction. The game has to make narrative sense for it to be enjoyable, and the structure has to be meaningful for maximal enjoyment. The parameters used to judge narrative pleasure in action games are, of course, other games, films and TV programmes. Gamesplayers are attuned to subtle differences in point of view and narrative coherence, some of which they typically articulate in language which recognizably belongs to media tradition: a first person shoot 'em up; a third person strategy adventure; a 3D action adventure. Some of the subgenres are classified, or clarified, through a new descriptive vocabulary, naming the structure, interface type or visual form: a point and click puzzle game, a platform game. Players can navigate this complex generic typology with ease, and assert a critical position, both personal and evidential, within their own 'great tradition'.

Narrative coherence is most important in roleplaying games (RPGs) and adventure games. Players of such games often seem more likely to operate against a literary framework, and most likely to articulate narrative concepts in their analysis of games and behaviour.

> *'I don't think that SoA has much replayability, but a great book (except for Lord of the Rings) needs at least a period of time between re-readings . . .'*
> 'the episodic format works very well for me, and it's nice to find a game with such a strong and interesting narrative drive.'
>
> (Users' comments on *Avalon 2000*)

The attraction of RPGs seems to be that of the fiction reader, vicarious exploration of the imagination of the other, and many players consequently seem to develop a substantial personal investment in these fictional worlds. This has been recognized by some researchers, and work has been done on building gaming environments with specific educational and literary aims in mind. The MUD (Multi-User Dungeon or Dimension) or MOO (MUD, Object Oriented) is a gaming environment in which players can wander and interact at will, either directing themselves to some explicit objective within that fantasy world (such as achieving a task, defined as in a conventional puzzle game) or addressing interactive objectives of their own. Many educational adaptations of this idea exist. For example, Holmevik and Haynes have developed 'the first publicly available MOO core database designed specifically for educational use' (Holmevik and Haynes 2000) and at the University of Bergen a MOO is being developed for teaching *Midsummer Night's Dream* (Bergen 1999).

A variant of the game between RPG and MUD is the interactive fiction. Some interactive fictions (IFs) are motivated by quite serious literary intent, such as the well respected work of Stuart Moulthrop and Michael Joyce (seminal works are Joyce 1990 and Moulthrop 1995). But the interactivity, puzzle element and non-linear multiple structures of such texts also can place them squarely in the game tradition. Siege of Avalon (the online RPG cited above) describes itself as 'a real-time "Traditional" medieval fantasy Role-Playing Game distributed as an Episodic Computer Game Novel™' (Avalon 2000). It is clearly intended as a game, and treated that way by its community, but is presented as a 'novel'.

A further variant of the interactive fiction is 'fanfiction'. Fanfictions fall into two types: those written by a single author, and those which are interactive, written by multiple authors, usually on the round-robin principle through email. Fanfictions are all inspired by popular culture artefacts, usually computer games, though sometimes by other fictions, such as anime comics.

Unlike MUDs these interactions are not the arbitrary inventions of the inhabitants of the MUD, they are strongly motivated by the narrative conventions, constraints and possibilities of the game: nothing can happen in the IF which is not plausible in game and narrative terms; plausibility is determined by the text's acceptability to the audience, who are themselves the other writers. This is not a minor hobby. One RPG webring records 216 fanfiction websites; a single one of those sites holds 250 fictions. (For examples of such fictions, inspired by the Final Fantasy game, see Final Fantasy 2000.)

So, at the same time as being an extension of the game, such an IF is also a piece of complex collaborative writing, in which authors represent characters. Here we have an example of writing which is taking place at quite a high level of sophistication, and has developed already an extensive popular tradition, *which would not exist without computer games.*

This desire to extend the gameplay into interactive verbal narrative is not limited to the specialist realm of interactive fiction, however. Game players in chatrooms are quite prepared to manufacture their own off-the-cuff virtual narratives. For example:

<NEMESIS>	im always following you loki
<Loki>	pulls out his rocket launcher
<NEMESIS>	where ever you go ill be behind you firing a rocket launcher
<Loki>	loads his ice rockets
<NEMESIS>	chuckles
<Loki>	and fire at NEMESIS
<Loki>	ha
<NEMESIS>	gets hit
<NEMESIS>	agh
<NEMESIS>	rooooaaaaaarrrrr!!!
<NEMESIS>	STARS!!!
<Loki>	reload quick
<Loki>	shit shit
<NEMESIS>	swings his fist and punches loki
<Loki>	fire fire
<Loki>	ouch
<Loki>	know my ass down
<NEMESIS>	throws loki to a wall

(Verbatim dialogue from Gamespy Arcade: Gamespy 1996)

This dialogue is virtual playground, spontaneous roleplay between two people who know nothing at all about each other, except that both are familiar with the computer game (and associated action movie) idiom. It is

not a sustained attempt at literary invention (unlike the aspirations of
many of the interactive fanfiction writers), it's merely knockabout
humour. At the same time, these players are generating dramatic dialogue,
complete with stage directions. Their knowledge of the conventions,
their sense of dramatic sequence, and their cooperative attempt to make
dramatic sense of the interaction, *through text*, even to creating a certain
tension as Loki panics, trying to load his gun before NEMESIS punches
him, and fails, is quite marked. I wonder if these same kids would create a
sequence like this if asked to write a drama in class.

In part players of computer games, and those who chat about such play,
are able to create such interactions, without thinking, because of the
strong intertextuality in their culture. They embed their gameplay in a
richer world of cultural allusion. This can be seen in the names chosen for
their personae in gameplay or chat and in the many references they make
directly or indirectly to fantasy, action and comic elements of popular
culture. In one half hour transcript there were references to Monty
Python, So I married an axe murderer, the Wizard of Oz, 'i live the smell of
napon (sic) in the morning', a Budweiser advertisement, an action film
and two popular songs.

Again it may be the mistaken preoccupation of educationalists with a
certain view of the literate that defines literacy inappropriately for modern
youth cultures, excluding such artefacts and so defining adolescent
expertise as non-literate. For example, literacy skills are needed when
young people decode the rules of a CCG and map them onto the 'reality'
of the film it is based on; or analyse the characterization in an RPG and
relate it to the comic book ('Buffy simply wouldn't be able to do that'); or
assess the impact of imagined worlds, their plausibility and emotive effects
('the Alien trilogy really scared me, much more than the film did'). All
of these demand skills of critical and evaluative reading, a knowledge of
popular texts, and an ability to present arguments which fit the netiquette
of the communicative medium, the expectations of the digital audience
in the aether and the constraints of keyboard, mouse and microphone.

Conclusion

Two conclusions seem possible from the discussion above. The first con-
clusion has to be that, by the traditional standards of literacy, we must
accept that some adolescents at least are developing their language
skills through their interaction with and around computer games. They
exhibit critical abilities, in their knowledge of and debate around genre
and narrative conventions. They exhibit creativity in the many different
contexts for the exploration and adaptation of language, including
the ability to generate new texts and multi-authored texts extending particular genres. Most importantly, they appear to deploy metalinguistic

knowledge, in their ability to refer to and to stand outside the linguistic devices they use.

However, a more radical suggestion is perhaps that the truly valuable knowledge such gamesplayers are acquiring, the multiplicity, complexity, social dependence and intertextuality of the language they use around computer games demands a more radical view of literacy than many educators are yet willing to give. In their exploration of new and widening modes of communication: in the multiple parallel skills needed to play a game and simultaneously deconstruct it online; in their willingness to collaborate, cooperate and communicate collectively; in creating interactive fan-fiction; in their readiness to acquire and evolve new codes, from the simplicity of emoticons to the netiquette of different flavours of chat; in the communicative flow across different media and different popular cultural forms, they are perhaps rapidly shifting modern modes of communication well beyond what can be serviced by conventional notions of 'good communication'.

Digital literacy acquired through computer games is increasingly social in both execution and articulation; and through the discourse of computer games (whether passively reporting them or actively engaged in them) kids may be acquiring modes of literacy which may be more relevant to future communicative needs than the traditional, print based modes which our educational practice focuses upon. Whilst there is no need to abandon the book, there is perhaps a need for the curriculum to embrace the digital text much more closely than it presently does, and perhaps to consider more directly the communicative value of the popular discourses that adolescents necessarily practise as part of their daily play.

References

Avalon (2000) *Siege of Avalon*, roleplaying game, http://www.siege-of-avalon.com/

Beavis, C. (1988) Pressing (the right?) buttons: literacy and technology, crisis and continuity, English in Australia, *The Journal of the Australian Association for the Teaching of English Inc.*, November: 123. http://www.aate.org.au/E_in_A/NOV%2098/983Beavis.html

Beavis, C. (1999) Magic or mayhem? New texts and new literacies in technological times. Paper presented at the Annual Conference of the Australian Association for Research in Education, Melbourne, Victoria, 28 November – 2 December. http://www.swin.edu.au/aare/99pap/bea99689.htm

Bergen (1999) *Midsummer Night's Dream: Literature on the Net, a Web and Moo Project at lingo.uib*. Bergen: Department of Humanistic Informatics, University of Bergen. html://cmc.uib.no/dream/index.html

Collot, M. and Belmore, N. (1996) Electronic language: a new variety of English, in Herring, S. (ed.), *Computer-mediated communication. Linguistic, social and cross-cultural perspectives*. Amsterdam and Philadelphia: John Benjamins.

Blanton, K. and Reiner, D. (1997) *Person to Person on the Internet*. London: AP Professional.

Final Fantasy (2000) http://members.tripod.com/~ArcanaTxM/frames.html
Gamespy Arcade (1996) http://www.gamespyarcade.com/
Gilster, Paul (1997) *Digital Literacy*. New York: John Wiley.
Hawisher, G. and Moran, C. (1997) The rhetorics and languages of electronic mail, in I. Snyder (ed.) *Page to Screen: Taking Literacy into the Electronic Era*. Sydney: Allen & Unwin.
Haynes, C., Holmevik, K. and Rune, J. (2000) *Lingua MOO: An Academic Virtual Community*, http://lingua.utdallas.edu/
Herring. S.C. (ed.) (1996) *Computer-mediated Communication: Linguistic, Social and Cross-cultural Perspectives*. Amsterdam: John Benjamins.
Hughes, S.K. and Shapiro, J.J. (1996) Information literacy as a liberal art, enlightenment proposals for a new curriculum, *Educom Review*, 31(2), http://www.educause.edu/pub/er/review/reviewArticles/31231.html
Joyce, M. (1990) *Afternoon, a Story, Hypertext Fiction*. Cambridge, MA: The Eastgate Press.
Kress, G. (1997) Visual and verbal modes of representation in electronically mediated communication: the potentials of new forms of text, in I. Snyder (ed.) *Page to Screen: Taking Literacy into the Electronic Era*. Sydney: Allen & Unwin.
Lea, M. (2000) Computer conferencing and assessment: new ways of writing in higher education. Paper delivered to American Educational Research Association, New Orleans, to be published in *Studies in Higher Education*.
Loa (2000) *Final Fantasy 7: Prophesy Fulfilled* an interactive fanfiction by 'Loa' http://shukumei.net/rpg/
Moulthrop, S. (1995) *Victory Garden, Hypertext Fiction*. Cambridge, MA: The Eastgate Press.
Sierra Games (1998) *Halflife*. Paris: Havas Interactive.
Silverblatt, A. (2000) Media literacy in the digital age. *Reading Online*, 4(3), available at: http://www.readingonline.org/newliteracies/lit_index.asp?HREF=/newliteracies/silverblatt/i
Snyder, I. (ed.) (1997) *Page to Screen: Taking Literacy into the Electronic Era*. Sydney: Allen & Unwin.
Warschauer, M. (1996) Comparing face-to-face and electronic discussion in the second language classroom. *CALICO Journal*, 13(2): 7–26. Also at http://www.lll.hawaii.edu/web/faculty/markw/comparing.html
Warschauer, M. (1997) A sociocultural approach to literacy and its significance for CALL, in K. Murphy and J. and R. Sanders (eds) *Nexus: The Convergence of Research and Teaching Through New Information Technologies*. Durham, NC: University of North Carolina.
Warschauer, M. (1999a) *Electronic Literacies: Language, Culture, and Power in Online Education*. Mahwah, NJ: Lawrence, Erlbaum Associates. Edited version of chapter 1 available at http://www.lll.hawaii.edu/web/faculty/markw/elec-intro.html.
Warschauer, M. (1999b) Millennialism and media: language, literacy, and technology in the 21st century. Keynote address delivered at the World Congress of Applied Linguistics (AILA), Tokyo, August. Available at: http://members.tripod.com/vstevens/papyrus/16sep99a.htm.
Werry, C.C. (1996) Linguistic and interactional features of Internet Relay Chat, *Herring*, pp. 47–63.

8

WHAT'S YOUR A/S/L? ELECTRONIC COMMUNICATION AND SYNCHRONOUS CHAT

Guy Merchant

... when you first start talking to them, if you type A/S/L that means age, sex, location and you type that and then they write like 15/f/US or something ...

Young people growing up with information technology are taking an active part in shaping new identities and developing new language forms. This teenager, in talking about her experience of communicating with 'virtual' friends in an internet chatroom, is explaining how the first marker of online identity is laid down in the context of a 'private chat' with another participant. 'What's your a/s/l?' is a conventional opening move in an innovative electronic genre which is highly interactive and increasingly popular with young people yet largely ignored in educational circles. Technically speaking, a chatroom is a form of synchronous computer-mediated communication. Synchronous communication requires participants to be online at the same time, taking part in an ongoing discussion in the form of rapid written conversation (Merchant 2001). A chat or IRC (internet relay chat) has the on-screen appearance of a play-script with each successive turn taking a new line on the screen. Successful online chat requires a basic working knowledge of ICT, confident keyboard skills and involves quite specific kinds of literacy.

IRCs are interesting for a number of reasons. First, they blur the distinction between speech and writing and as such constitute a new and developing linguistic form (Merchant 2001). The need for rapid conversational turn-taking between geographically remote participants encourages innovation in the ways that writing is used to do conversational work. So, for example, because the contextual and paralinguistic information available in face-to-face interaction is not present, users have to resort to new iconic and symbolic conventions to supply information on such matters as seriousness, emphasis, surprise and so on. Second, because the IRC format encourages rapid response, participants work quickly to secure their turn and message content becomes more important than surface polish. As a result grammatical completeness, spell-checking and proof-reading are redundant. Third, the identity of participants is always uncertain. It is assumed that they are usually geographically dispersed (although still very present in the moment of communication) but this is seldom verifiable. IRC users can never be absolutely sure that their 'friends' are who they say they are or even where they say they are, unless of course they are sitting beside each other in a computer lab or internet cafe. Because the identity of participants is always uncertain, clues in the form of nicknames (nicks), information on personal profiles and related web pages, as well as hints about interests (such as favourite TV programmes or recording artists) are important. In addition to this both conversational topics and the language used to express them become salient markers of identity.

Teenagers frequently report on their use of abbreviations (for example, ROTFL – roll on the floor laughing), punctuation and capitalization in giving additional 'colour' to their chat.

You can like shout at people in chat – you can use capitals if you're in an annoyed mood.

Some of these innovations are beginning to cross between media, showing up in text-messaging, advertising and even the writing of younger children.

In the following extract a 7-year-old boy develops action and excitement in a sci-fi story through a now familiar experimentation with print features. His story is word-processed and this clearly alerts him to new possibilities.

Bang!! 'wow!!!' aaaaaaaaaaaaaah went the siren 'wow what's going on' buzzzzzz control buzzzzzz failing buuuuuzzzzzzzzzz 'take cover' bang!!

This episode is embedded in a sophisticated narrative but here it is used to highlight the sort of language changes that new technology is encouraging. As we shall see, conservative critics are concerned about these changes but in doing so they may simply be attempting to re-establish control through complaint.

Tasteful or what?

The question of how to respond to popular culture is a problem that educationists frequently wrestle with (Marsh and Millard 2001). The social practices and textual forms that characterize young people's interactions in the new communication landscape are an aspect of popular culture that provokes heated debate in the media and in educational discourse (Hunt 2000). Uncertainties about the relationship between popular culture and mainstream schooling are accompanied by concerns about language change or 'verbal hygiene' (Cameron 1995). Bourdieu (1992) argues that popular speech, like popular culture or popular music, is always defined in relation to the dominant and dominating form. Popular speech, he argues, is that which is excluded from the legitimate language: the language inculcated by various agencies – including the school system. Consequently, our pre-occupation with promoting a narrowly-defined version of literacy in the school system (what Bourdieu calls 'legitimate language') leads us to demonize new language and new language users. The following extract from the *Times Educational Supplement* illustrates this tendency:

> The trend for ditching grammar, spelling and vowels in emails and mobile-phone text messages could undermine attempts to improve pupils' writing. Without teachers and parents to regulate new modes of communication, children are replacing time-consuming, properly constructed language with a quick-fire mix of letters, numbers and punctuation.
>
> (*TES* 2000)

Here, the author argues that teachers and parents should be regulators, emphasizing the importance of 'properly constructed language' – in other words that they should be inculcators of the legitimate language (Bourdieu 1992: 62). Yet even if they could regulate the new modes of communication, would this be appropriate? Or does the argument simply set up an unhelpful opposition between different kinds of literacy? This is an extract from an email written by a high-achieving English graduate:

> Dear L, sorry I've been soooooo shit at replying, but still can't figure out how to get into my college email system from home (durrr-computer virgin!-well not really they just seem to have made it really difficult) and have been in school full time. As for chilling at at half term – what

f*cking half term!! Yes, theoretically my school was on half term . . . my whole family (all teachers/pupils) were half-terming it – B*STARDS!
(Dickinson and Merchant 2001)

This text exhibits some of the linguistic features that are beginning to be identified in popular electronic texts. The author uses vowel reduplication for emphasis 'soooooo', capitalization and cartoon-like exclamations 'DURRR-COMPUTER VIRGIN'. Such language use is highly controversial. Some commentators in the 'complaint tradition' (Milroy and Milroy 1985) claim that language is being corrupted, whilst others are excited by this new direction in language change. In this vein, researchers such as Werry (1996), Morgan and Hawisher (1998), Shortis (2001), and Merchant (2001) draw attention to the creativity of this evolving language showing how it functions as a highly effective medium of communication in the everyday lives of many teenagers and young people.

Young teenagers appear to be playing a key role in the linguistic innovation associated with the new communication technology. They draw freely from popular culture creating a 'bricolage of discursive fragments drawn from songs, TV characters and a variety of different social speech types' (Werry 1996: 58) and are constructing relationships, social practices and texts that are 'blended, merged and reshaped' (Luke 2000: 77). Language features are borrowed and adapted to explore the possibilities and limitations of the different communication media. In doing this, young language users are appropriating language forms and populating them with their own intentions (Bakhtin 1998: 293).

The chatroom environment

Technically speaking, a chatroom is a form of computer-mediated communication. The synchronous nature of this communication requires participants to be online at the same time. Unlike a bulletin board or an email there is usually no way of sending a message that is read later on. Chat happens in the 'now', in real time, even though participants may be inhabiting different time zones. However, because the screen reveals lines of text sequentially, there is a brief time delay which often creates a multi-stranded conversation with some participants responding to earlier turns whilst others are developing a new topic thread (see Crystal 2001).

The extract below is an example of a relatively focused chat between five participants. A university tutor (A) is encouraging students (B, C, E and D) to reflect on their science teaching.

A: I am a firm believer that there is very little that children can discover
    – teachers need to put them in a position of tripping over ideas and
    expereinces and then helping them to make sense of them

C: on Thursday this week – I am having my 3rd science lesson on Electricity – and we have covered the basics and simple circuits etc – so I have designed some challenge sheets to make light houses, wind mills etc – using the same basic

B: Vygotsky?

E: -not connected – regarding spreadsheets – will the children eventually design them to record their findings or do we do the donkey work?

C: concepts with circuits – just modifying things – cos my focus is to let the children experiment

D: what age is this?

A: Vygotsky suggests that perople operate in socity terms and not merely as individuals

D: philosophy as well as science just as well I've got coffee

Chatroom extract

Despite the fact that all five are talking about science teaching, the conversation is disjointed and multi-stranded. 'A' introduces ideas about learning theory which are actually picked up by 'B' in the third turn and then returned to again later on by 'A'. At the same time, however, 'C' and 'E' are reporting on practical experiences. The participant 'D' successfully manages to bridge both strands with relatively brief contributions to the ongoing conversations.

Most open access chatrooms – the sort that are popular with teenagers – involve more participants who take shorter conversational turns. The result is more chaotic: there are more strands and less overall coherence. Some commentators have observed that this sort of chat has many of the features of a noisy party. So, in order to move away from the chatroom 'noise' participants may choose a private (one-to-one) chat or move to another 'room'.

Figure 8.1 is a screen-shot of a chatroom regularly visited by two teenage girls in an earlier study (Merchant 2001). Even for those familiar with web pages, this is a complex screen – and it is worth bearing in mind that it is only one of a number of chat environments used by some of the teenagers. A brief analysis of the page may be helpful at this point. For those with some familiarity with the appearance of a web page, the top and bottom 'bars', although loaded with information of various kinds, are usually ignored when using the page. The specific design of the page (its distinguishing features) are the windows within this frame. Immediately underneath the Freeserve navigation bar is the chatroom identification which tells us that we are in the 'Bored Room (nothin' to do nothin' to say)' at Yahoo! Chat. Below are windows showing the chat itself and the participants' onscreen identity (e.g.: wickedklowngirl 2001) and beneath this is the user's chatbox in which she enters her contribution. The rest of the screen is fairly straight forward, but

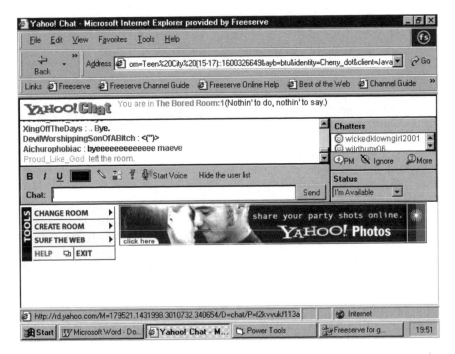

Figure 8.1   The Yahoo! Chat Environment

it is worth noting that it includes access to tools for changing and creating rooms.

At this point, it is perhaps important to recognize a major limitation of the screenshot – the page is not static. In an IRC, the conversation evolves over time, the participants change and the user has a number of ways of interacting with and making changes to the screen page. The chat page has a complex verbal and visual design, yet many teenagers are highly skilled at moving between rooms, scrolling through the list of participants and changing the size and shape of windows (for example to make ongoing chat take up more of the screen space). Apart from this, in order to fully participate, they need to read quickly and respond without too much hesitation. High levels of concentration are required to stay with a chat, users become very involved and can monopolize available online time. Morgan and Hawisher (1998) suggest that this is why many American universities have banned the use of IRCs at public computer sites and Werry (1995) goes as far as to suggest that chat can be addictive.

Some teenage girls report that they regularly visit chatrooms, whilst others are familiar with chat environments but consider themselves to be 'occasional' visitors. More regular participants may make use of an online pager to establish contact with 'friends':

R: you can look for them because I get messages from people on my
     pager thing.
I: So you know there in there . . . and then in the chatroom you can
     talk to everybody can you?
S: Yeah, you can . . .
I: . . . and then you can come out . . .
S: . . . and have private chats with other people . . .
I: yeah, yeah . . . so how do you choose to do that?
S: You say does anyone want to chat to . . .
R: . . . either they send you a little message – you know a little extra box
     – either they send it to you or you double-click and you can send
     one to them.

Interview extract

The teenage girls in my study expressed a preference for chat environments that are predominantly verbal, although there had been some
experimentation with the more visual chatrooms in which participants
are represented by on-screen icons or avatars. IRCs with avatars still enjoy
considerable popularity on the internet, but this network of teenagers felt
that they 'got boring' and that they 'didn't have enough rooms'.

Who's there?

Young people's use of chatrooms opens up the possibility of communication with an extended group of 'friends'. The communicative audience
is varied. Not only can a chatroom introduce another channel of communication with an existing friendship group (locally, nationally or
internationally) but it also extends the social network to include those
who they have not met and are unlikely to meet in a face-to-face situation.
I refer to the former as 'actual friends' and the latter as 'virtual friends'
but will suggest later that these need not be seen as stable or watertight
categories.

Chatroom use in this age group was normally restricted to informal
social interaction and included a varied audience. Some of the girls saw
chatrooms as places where they could meet both actual and virtual friends.
Virtual contacts might be added to the user's list of 'personal friends', most
of whom they were unlikely to meet in 'real life'. Online observations
showed frequent use of aliases through which chatroom participants
may provide hints about their actual or fictional identity (e.g.: 'pintsize' or
'cherry-dot').

The interviewees in my study did not express any particularly strong
interest in internet romance, but given their relationship to the inter-
viewer this was obviously a difficult area to explore. However, one
interviewee did describe how she had made a virtual friend through a

Dreamcast internet chat. She later discovered that he lived locally and agreed to meet up with him (this meeting was carefully monitored by the girl's parents). So, although face-to-face meeting is always possible (as it is with pen-pals) it was not seen by the other girls as a normal outcome of online interaction. Virtual friends may or may not become actual friends.

In chatrooms, users may have regular virtual friends but several of the interviewees claimed that they would sometimes 'meet up' with actual friends either by chance or by arrangement. The interviewees in this study talked about 'meeting up' with friends from school in chatrooms:

> R: Sometimes . . . people suddenly send you a message and you say 'Oh, I think I know you'.
> I: Mm
> S: . . . or you can say: meet me online at 6 o'clock.
> R: Yeah.
> I: OK – do you ever do that?
> R: Yes

Interview extract

Here the fluidity of communication becomes apparent. An online meeting may be arranged in a face-to-face meeting or via a phone call or text message. One of the girls described how she liked to have her mobile phone to hand whilst visiting a chatroom so that she didn't 'miss anything'.

As chatroom use increases it may be that the distinction between actual and virtual friends begins to break down – all participants are reduced to their on-screen utterances, alias or web persona in a sequential flow of online conversation. For some of these teenagers, there was a sense in which they were beginning to build a relationship with internet friends who they regularly met online and had been added to their personal lists. The following interview extracts show the interviewees exploring the concept of internet friends and moving towards the idea of a distinct communicative setting: cyberspace.

> I: Do you find the same people?
> N: Yeah you can save them as friends and then when you get to go on it tells you if they're on.
> I: So have you got some friends?
> [. . .]
> N: Yeah, I've got about fifty.
> I: About fifty! Fifty friends.
> H: She's more popular than me [joking].
> N: . . . on the list, and when I go on it tells you if they're on or not . . . if one of them's on then I'll talk to them . . .

[. . .]
I: Do you feel you know them at all though?
N: [chuckles]
I: . . . like from one – when you log on one time to the next . . .
N: Well, some people – it depends.
[. . .]
I: Do you ever wish you could really meet them? Or do you just think of them as like . . .
H: Not really real.
I: Not real people?
N: No.
I: No?
N: They're just in cyberspace.

Interview extract

It is interesting to note that in this and other discussions chatroom users tended to view their virtual friends as partly fictitious. They are 'not really real' – yet when asked if they believed in the stated identity of a virtual friend, interviewees claimed they saw no reason why someone in a chatroom would experiment, change or conceal their real identity. Turkle's (1995) observation that electronic communication allows users to play different roles or create 'online selves' may well be true, but this sort of experimentation did not seem to make sense to these teenagers. 'What would be the point?' one commented when asked if she had ever pretended to be someone else when online. Perhaps this is a reflection of this particular age or gender group who may be too pre-occupied with establishing and confirming their own identity in relation to their peer-group to try on different identities. Of course others in the chatroom may be creative in describing their own age, sex and interests but this did not appear to bother these girls at all.

Talking in writing

The challenge of representing chat – usually a conversational form – in writing means that participants need to be innovative in linguistic terms but also willing to share and pass on these innovations. Other studies, based on larger samples of chat data, suggest that quite specific linguistic features are being developed to substitute for paralinguistic and prosodic features, actions and gestures (see Werry 1996). Observations in this study showed frequent use of features like vowel reduplication, expletives, non-standard punctuation, and capitalization. Abbreviations and emoticons were also regularly used.

In the following extract, the interviewee R (using her chatroom alias 'pintsize') enters into a private chat with a virtual friend (alias 'adz46'):

```
adz46:      hows you
pintsize:   fine thanx u?
adz46:      great
pintsize:   cool wot u up2?
adz46:      not A LOT
pintsize:   wot av u bin up2?
adz46:      Writeing a Macbeth Essay
pintsize:   o gr8 fun!
adz46:      mmmmmmm
adz46:      :-(
pintsize:   :)
adz46:      :-(
pintsize:   cheer up!
adz46:      :-|
pintsize:   Stop it!
[interaction ends]
```
Chatroom conversation

Here, the supportive tone is provided by punctuation and the use of emoticons, which substitute for some of the paralinguistic features that one might expect in a similar face-to-face interaction. The creative phonic spelling ('thanx' and 'wot'), slang ('cool') and abbreviations (gr8) that are used here are also a distinctive feature of many IRCs.

Commentators have suggested that kinds of specialized chat language can be used to exclude the uninitiated (Abbott 1998). The teenagers in this study did not think that this was the case, arguing that most communication problems are rapidly resolved:

I: So what do you do if you don't know [what they mean]
A: I just ask them . . . what do you mean when you say . . . whatever.
Interview extract

So more experienced users do not appear to exercise power or exclusion through their use of jargon. In fact my study suggests that abbreviations are exchanged and developed on a regular basis.

N: You shorten everything . . . yeah?
I: Do you?
N: Abbreviations.
I: Like what?
H: BRB
I: What's that?
H: Be right back.
I: Oh right any others?

N: ... and LOL – laughing out loud
  [...]
I: Do you ... how do you learn all those?
H: ... I don't know – you just go oh what's that ...
N: ... you just pick them up. If somebody does them you say what does that mean and also ... like everything ... 'cause it's different like if you're saying 'before' you'd just write 'B4'

Interview extract

These language features are common to email correspondence, text-messaging and chatroom interaction and all participants reported some knowledge of them. These abbreviations can be roughly categorized into four types (see Figure 8.2). First those that use non-alphabetic characters to construct icons – usually relating to emotions (hence the coinage: emoticon); second, simple abbreviation in which initial letters are used as shorthand (this of course builds on an established tradition in intimate letter writing, such as the use of SWALK for 'sealed with a loving kiss'); third, combinations of numbers and letters to create an approximate phonetic rendering of the message (for example 'NE1' for anyone) and fourth, phonetic spelling. In some cases these users would combine elements from different categories in a single message.

Use of non-alphabetic characters (emoticons) Read with one's head inclined to the left	:-)	happy
	;-)	wink
	:-}	embarassed
	\~~~/	food
	#-)	partied all night
Use of initial letter abbreviation	AFAIK	as far as I know
	BTW	by the way
	ROTFL	rolling on the floor laughing
	JAM	just a minute
	IDK	I don't know
Phonetic representation using numbers and letters	GR8	great
	NE1	anyone
	BCNU	be seeing you
	CUL8R	see you later
	2NITE	tonight
Phonetic spelling	BUK	book
	WOZ	was
	AV	have
	WOT	what
	CUM	come

Figure 8.2   Categories of abbreviation used in electronic communication

Although plenty of guidance on the conventions of online interaction or 'netiquette' is available, most of these users reported that they learnt the rules of the game through first hand experience, from friends or occasionally through the magazines they read. One of the interviewees in this study referred to information gained from computer games magazines whilst another used teenage magazines like '19' to collect chatroom tips and useful websites. But it also seems that language features are regularly transferred between different media – song lyrics, adverts, TV, magazines, text messages – in other words across the whole field of popular culture. So, for example, the opener 'Whaaaaasup?' (What's up?) popularized by the mobile phone conversation in the Budweiser TV advert uses the same vowel reduplication found in the closing 'byeeeeeeeeeeeeee!' and the magazine *Celebrity Looks* (August 2001: 97): 'This black and white top is soooo sexy, I love it!'

Another distinctive feature of computer-mediated communication is the way in which it allows rapid and flexible movement between different formats. In chatrooms these participants often asked each other for picture files and sometimes exchanged personal website addresses. If either or both of the users have their own web page, interaction may involve an exchange of URLs. From time to time they would include URLs of their favourite sites such as those of recording artists or other popular icons in their ongoing conversations.

In the example below 'cherry-dot' (H's online alias) invites a chatroom participant into a one-to-one interaction. After exchanging a/s/l (age/sex/location) they begin a conversation about 'mullets' – the ridiculed, short-at-the front and long-at-the back hairstyle fashionable in the 1970s.

hoopy_da_hula:	yeh!
hoopy_da_hula:	19/m/uk
hoopy_da_hula:	bus driver has the best mullet!
hoopy_da_hula:	bald on top, 12inches long at the back. tasteful
cherry_dot:	oh thats good check out www.mullet.co.uk
hoopy_da_hula:	you?
cherry_dot:	16/f/England
hoopy_da_hula:	where in england?
cherry_dot:	Sheffield
hoopy_da_hula:	bristol
cherry_dot:	cool
cherry_dot:	how are you then?
hoopy_da_hula:	nice pics, btw![btw = by the way]
cherry_dot:	oh thanx!
cherry_dot:	hello?
cherry_dot:	r u still there?

Chatroom conversation

During this interaction, picture files and websites were exchanged and the participants demonstrated the ability to move quickly between web page windows and chat texts without interrupting the flow of conversation. Whilst the conversation is informal, short and tentative in nature it does point to the potential of computer-based communication and the ways in which some teenagers are developing a range of important skills that are often not acknowledged in educational settings.

All fingers and thumbs

When teenagers are online they are learning a whole range of new literacy skills. At a very basic level they are developing a fluency in mouse and keyboard control, motivated by a drive to maintain the pace or conversational flow of chatroom interaction. They are also involved in experimentation with abbreviation and the use of non-alphabetic keyboard symbols. At the same time they are becoming confident at navigating across quite complex screens, moving between several windows and incorporating hyperlinks in the texts they use. But perhaps the most significant development is the exploration of a new kind of communication – an emerging electronic genre that I have described as a written conversation – one in which writing acts in ways normally associated with the spoken word. As computer conferencing becomes more widespread, in administration, business and online learning these early experiments in chat may well take on a new significance.

The young people who have access to new technology are active agents in a developing linguistic market (Bourdieu 1992) but the value of their exchanges are de-limited by its relationship to the wider social habitus. The association of chatroom interaction with the 'informal', the 'frivolous', and the 'social' helps to define their position in a language hierarchy. However, powerful forces are at work as on one hand commercial and global forces seek to commodify new language codes (Orange 2000) whilst on the other hand, traditionally dominant groups seek to reinforce the norms of legitimate language.

I have argued that through their experimentation with the new communication media, the same young people who are seen as being at risk through their aberrant use of language are actually developing very marketable skills, which may in themselves become capital in a new technologized social order. However, since home access during leisure time seems to be a significant setting in which to develop these skills those growing up in professional and middle class families (in other words, those most likely to have internet access) may well be at an advantage.

The field of new communication can be seen as a site in which a complex struggle for domination is in progress. The forces of an emergent global culture, supported by commercial interests, are pitted against the more conservative forces of the education system and other agents of language control. Although there are moves to harness the learning potential of ICT in schools, and calls to acknowledge the literacy practices of adolescents (O'Brien, Moje and Stewart 2001) concerns over standards of writing have, as we have seen, been linked to the corrupting influence of new media (see Luke and Luke 2001 for a more thorough exploration of this). Recent moves to reinstate formal grammar in the school curriculum in England (Myhill 1999; DfEE 2000) suggest an attempt to innoculate the young against this new danger. This is seen by Bourdieu as a classic way in which the education system contributes to the maintenance of habitus:

> Through its grammarians, who fix and codify legitimate usage and its teachers who impose and inculcate it through numerous acts of correction, the education system tends, in this area as elsewhere, to produce the need for its own products, ie the labour and instruments of correction.
>
> (Bourdieu 1992: 60–1)

There is no doubt that the language changes explored in this chapter are a powerful force in the contemporary world. I have argued that popular electronic and digital communication, particularly as used by young people, is becoming a site of struggle in which existing forms of linguistic capital are challenged. This is not problematic to the young, who as we have seen are the innovators, but to those who claim to have their best interests at heart and must somehow resolve the tension between a traditional view of language and the need to respond to economic and social change.

Despite political encouragement to develop the use of new technology in the classroom (for example BECTA 2001) educational thinking about ICT is plagued by contradiction. Electronic communication, computer ownership and internet access are increasingly widespread and popular, yet we are reluctant to value the skills and knowledge that pupils develop outside the classroom. Rather than drawing on their experience we problematize popular forms focusing our anxieties on the alienated adolescent 'techno-subject'. As Luke and Luke observe:

> Variously labelled Generation-X, web surfies, screenagers, digikids, techno-kids or cyberpunks, by the end of the millenium, computer savvy cybernaughts had left parents and teachers behind in the emerging generational-digital divide.
>
> (Luke and Luke 2001: 103)

Since the early introduction of computers in schools we have tried to regulate and 'dignify' the use of technology. Perhaps the most dominant educational practices have involved little more than cosmetic changes to the development of traditional print literacy. This has resulted in over-valuing word-processing and keyboard skills and the denigration of popular thumb-controlled technology (associated with games consoles, joysticks, and more recently with text-messaging). New electronic communication in the form of emails, chatrooms and mobile phones now span this divide. If we are to encourage our pupils to develop the communication skills that they will need in both private and public life in the twenty-first century we need a more creative response to popular forms.

References

Abbot, C. (1998) Making connections: young people and the Internet, in J. Sefton-Green (ed.) *Digital Diversions: Youth Culture in the Age of Multimedia*. London: UCL Press.

Bakhtin, M.M. (1998) *The Dialogic Imagination*. Austin: University of Texas.

British Educational Communications and Technology Agency (BECTA) (2001) *Building the Grid: Aims of the NGfL Online*. http://becta.org.uk/buildingthegrid/ngflaims.html (accessed 6 July 2001).

Bourdieu, P. (1992) *Language and Symbolic Power*. Cambridge: Polity Press.

Cameron, D. (1995) *Verbal Hygiene*. London: Routledge.

Chun, D. (1994) Using computer networking to facilitate the acquisition of interactive competence, *System*, 22(1):17–31.

Crystal, D. (2001) *Language and the Internet*. Cambridge: Cambridge University Press.

Davis, B., Sanger, J., Willson, J. and Whittaker, R. (1997) *Young Children, Videos and Computer Games – Issues for Teachers and Parents*. London: Falmer Press.

Department for Education and Employment (DfEE) (2000) *Grammar for Writing*. London: HMSO.

Dickinson, P. and Merchant, G. (2001) Literacy and computer mediated communication – a case study of web-based teacher training. Paper presented to the 8th International Literacy and Education Conference.

Henry, J. (2000) E-mail is:-, for writing, *Times Education Supplement*, 1 September, p. 22.

Hunt, P. (2000) Futures for children's literature: evolution or radical break? *Cambridge Journal of Education*, 30(1): 111–19.

Kaplan, N. and Farrell, E. (1994) Weavers of webs: a portrait of young women on the net, *Arachnet Electronic Journal of Virtual Culture*, 2: 3.

Kress, G. (1998) Visual and verbal modes of representation in electronically mediated communication: the potentials of new forms of texts, in I. Snyder (ed.) *Page to Screen: Taking Literacy into the Electronic Era*. London: Routledge.

Luke, A. and Luke, C. (2001) Adolescence lost/childhood regained: on early intervention and the emergence of the techno-subject, *Journal of Early Childhood Education*, 1(1): 91–120.

Luke, C. (2000) Cyberschooling and technological change: multiliteracies for new times, in B. Cope and M. Kalantzis (eds) *Multiliteracies – Literacy Learning and the Design of Social Futures*. South Yarra: Macmillan.

Merchant, G. (2001) Teenagers in cyberspace: language use and language change in internet chatrooms, *Journal of Research in Reading*, 24(3): 293–306.

Milroy, J. and Milroy, L. (1985) *Authority in Language*. London: Routledge and Kegan Paul.

Morgan, C. and Hawisher, G. (1998) The rhetorics and language of e-mail, in I. Snyder (ed.) *Page to Screen – Taking Literacy into the Electronic Era*. London: Routledge.

Myhill, D. (1999) Writing matters: linguistic characteristics of writing in GCSE English examinations, *English in Education*, 33(3): 70–81.

O'Brien, D.G., Moje, E.B. and Stewart, R.A. (2001) Exploring the context of secondary literacy in pupils everyday social lives, in E.B. Moje and D.G. O'Brien (eds) *Constructions of Literacy*. New Jersey: Lawrence Erlbaum Associates.

Orange (2000) *Just Talk*, publicity booklet. Bristol: Orange Personal.

Shortis, T. (2001) *The Language of ICT*. London: Routledge.

Turkle, S. (1995) *Life on Screen: Identity in the Age of the Internet*. New York: Simon and Schuster.

Werry, C. (1996) Linguistic and interactional features of internet relay chat, in S.C. Herring (ed.) *Computer-Mediated Communication: Linguistic, Social and Cross-cultural Perspectives*. Amsterdam: Benjamins.

Whitehouse, C. (1995) Refashioning boys' toys, *Times Higher Educational Supplement*, 12 May.

Introduction to Chapter 9

IS OPEN CENSORSHIP A REQUIRED TEACHING AND LEARNING STRATEGY?

Moira Monteith

There is an important point to bear in mind in introducing this chapter: the question as to whether or not there is a 'moral dimension' to literacy or do we consider it in school as merely a set of skills to be acquired. Since most of us would censor some materials in an attempt to safeguard our pupils from negative or problem items, it seems there must be a dimension other than that of skills acquisition.

Contributors to this book argue that the concept of literacy is still evolving and ICT has moved 'literacy' on in terms of its communication and application. In turn, this latest literacy technology, ICT, has resulted in easy access to problematic material. Has literacy always had a negative side?

When Richard Hoggart wrote his outstanding critique of literacy in the age of mass communication and state provision of education, he shrewdly named his book: *The Uses of Literacy*. In a few sections of the book, he revealed the downside of mass literacy which he claimed ranged from smutty stories with crude drawings handed around by working class men in factories to what might be called the gutter press, with reliance on sensational items and the presentation of difficult and complex arguments in a simplistic manner. When we consider the uses of the internet we need to be aware of the prevalence of pornography on a very much wider scale than many of us had ever imagined as well as internet chatlines where the grooming of young children is by no means uncommon. There are more ICT contaminations than computer viruses. A few are to do with forces unleashed from somewhere deep within the human psyche. In the secondary curriculum it is surely part of the teaching remit to make our students aware of the negative side of communication technologies and to discuss this openly.

Nowadays we can exclude visits to undesirable websites quite easily. However, it is difficult to ensure this is always the case, for example in home use. Some sites obtrude on our awareness unsought. For example, a teacher who was organizing a lesson for his class in 1998, before many schools had their own firewall systems in operation, presented a version of this lesson first to a group of teachers on an internet course. As we followed his demonstration, he clicked on a website brought up by the search engine about planets (on which the lesson was based). He clicked the website URL next to the one intended, an easy slip of the mouse. The title included the word planet and was indeed very harmless sounding. It happened to be a porn site. He was extremely relieved that he had tried the lesson out on us first, but the problem still remained. Sometimes undesirable sites are clever at hiding what they are. Other pupils might easily click on the site while following perfectly reasonable instructions about web searches.

Searching for information with unpleasant aspects or details is hardly new. At a conference some years ago librarians said they had begun to buy paperbacks (instead of hardback editions) for school libraries of books consistently stolen. One such book concerned the history of the Third Reich, with details of death camps. Librarians doubted these texts were stolen to revise for exams or for other scholarly purposes, whether or not they were on teachers' reading lists. Now it is far easier to find 'inappropriate' as well as appropriate information on the web, for instance sites on cannibalism and torture or instructions on making bombs.

The 'negative' side to literacy may include what we choose to read or view. In a later book, Hoggart states that 'a line of dates, chosen almost at random' can 'make many feel uneasy'. He suggests one such line: 'the 1870 Elementary Education Act; the assertion in the final decade of the nineteenth century that Britain, the first nation to be able to make the claim, was a substantially literate country; the 1944 Education Act, the Open University of 1969 . . . and today the *Sun*' (Hoggart, 1996: 21). He suggests as a remedy: 'Down with subliteracy, up with critical literacy.' Discriminating language analysis is surely a fundamental part of any literacy expertise higher than basic skills in reading and writing. There have been plenty of books for English teachers in the past as well as the present, which define such higher level skills. Previously, it was difficult to focus on critical literacy fully within the classroom owing to a lack of current newspapers or a wide range of texts or the ability to discuss radio and TV versions in conjunction with other texts. With the use of ICT we may well have the context and the tools in the classroom for the first time to help students gain higher level analytic skills. In that case, one result will be a consideration of exactly what is happening on the internet and in electronic communication.

The effects of ICT can penetrate society insidiously or positively depending on the context and your point of view. They are even more challenging than the onset of mass literacy beginning in the early years of the twentieth century.

The camera as a tool and a medium has merged with the computer, creating an even more compelling, and disconcertingly complex set of challenges and opportunities for discovering and exploring the traditional distinctions between data and information, information and knowledge, knowledge and wisdom (Marcus 2000: 42).

As literacy itself evolves and our applications of it change via texts, film, phones and computers, any analysis changes also. Though, as Marcus says, the *traditional* areas of data, information, knowledge and wisdom remain. Our remit probably cannot aspire to the acquisition of wisdom, but we should be able to encourage our pupils to gain a level of basic literacy skills + a level of discriminating knowledge analysis. From that, wisdom may follow with experience. The following definitions from the Concise Oxford Dictionary may help us, in discussion with our students, in deciding how we categorize literacy activities.

Data	Noun plural (also treated as singular as in *that is all the data we have*)
1	known facts or things used as a basis for inference or reckoning
2	quantities or characters operated on by a computer etc.
	databank a store or source of data
	data capture the action or process of entering data into a computer
	data processing a series of operations on data, esp. by a computer, to retrieve or classify information
	data processor a machine, especially a computer, that carries out data processing

Information	
1	something told, knowledge
2	usually followed by *on, about* items of knowledge, news

Knowledge	
1a	(usually followed by *of*) awareness or familiarity gained by experience (of a person, fact or thing) (*there is no knowledge of that*)
1b	a person's range of information (*is not within his/her knowledge*)
2a	(usually followed by *of*) a theoretical or practical understanding of a subject, language etc (*has a good knowledge of Greek*)
2b	the sum of what is known (*every branch of knowledge*)
3 *Philos.*	true, justified belief; certain understanding as opposed to opinion.

Wisdom
1   the state of being wise
2   experience and knowledge together with the power of applying them
        critically or practically
3   sagacity, prudence, common sense
        wise sayings, thoughts etc to be regarded collectively

NB wise   having experience and knowledge and judiciously applying them
        US colloq. **get wise to** become aware of

Will discussion of 'data and information, information and knowledge, knowledge and wisdom' bring us any nearer to a critical consideration of the internet and its open sesame cave of information? As Sue Brindley says in Chapter Two, 'one of the main purposes of literacy is to understand how language and image can be used to control'. It is useful to consider both control and exploitation when analysing all forms of literacy. Oral language can control, incite, frighten, exclude, include and so on. Hitler's speeches may seem overdramatic and slightly grotesque nowadays but in the diaries of young soldiers and pilots at the time, it is clear they were fired by enthusiasm after hearing him. More recently, in Ruanda, the genocide was preceded by days of ranting on the radio inciting hatred towards one group of people.

Visual material can be equally powerful and a dominant usage may be subverted. In the International Center of Photography in New York alongside an exhibition of photographs of the September 11th disaster a year after the event, there was a room given over to photography by Afghan women (The Revolutionary Association of the Women of Afghanistan). The women had hidden still and video cameras under their burqas to film what was happening to them as women. They were careful to stress in an accompanying commentary that the ill treatment handed out to them by the Taliban was only a more severe and public version of ill treatment suffered by many generations of women in Afghanistan. Their photos showed women being beaten by truncheons for wearing garments that revealed their ankles and women being shot for alleged adultery in public executions on football fields. They included pictures of women and children dead and maimed from the allied bombing in 2002. The cameras were being used in part to subvert a hideous sense of control. By critiquing a wide range of texts and images, our students and pupils can gain considerably in deciding the importance of context, medium and language used.

Finally, it seems that the struggle to safeguard our pupils and ourselves from undesirable material is continuous. Ingenious leap-frogging goes on between regulators and those who break the regulations. Currently, unlooked for messages can arrive via spam. Much of this spam is inherently annoying if not downright unpleasant. Bill Gates stated

25 January 2004 that Microsoft will attempt to get rid of spam within two years and other software managers and internet service providers (ISPs) have begun to do this already.

Here is someone's current (December 2003) thoughts on spam:

Spam, I must admit, is utterly fascinating. While it is truely annoying, it's amazing to see the lengths that people will go to in order to get around spam filters, and catch peoples attention. Misleading subject lines (we all know that one), misspelled words. common words, with spaces or * or other characters in them. Special chars to replace common letters (1 for l, @ for a, and so on . . .), spam about not getting any more spam (I love that one).

Is anybody actually making money off of spam? Or is it the same myth that chain letters use, the somebody got rich off the letter, but theoretically, by the time you send it out, you haven't made any money at all, but spent quite a lot . . .

(OT: MadLibs spam)

Complete safety is never possible. However much we safeguard young users some awfulness may wriggle through. The ability and ingenuity of some IT users to break into others' privacy seems amazing. Perhaps it shouldn't come as a surprise to find that if people can hack into websites such as the Pentagon that they can also get into individual email message boxes.

Skills are skills and perhaps can be taught as skills from generation to generation. But if we don't deal with the context in which those skills are used, then we are hardly helping our students effectively to deal with today's literacy let alone tomorrow's. The following chapter deals with information from a specific set of families and their attitudes towards their children's use of the internet at home. These parents were aware of the challenges brought by use of ICT but there is a disparity between parental views and their actual implementation. Using this material, a data snapshot, we can begin to plan our own approaches in and out of school.

A society such as this needs, not what it largely has today, an inadequately literate, comprehensively abused majority, but a critically literate majority . . . One has all the time to be working towards an open society capable of respecting and using its openness in the right ways . . .

(Hoggart 1996: 301)

Most teachers and parents, I am convinced, wish to encourage an open society and not become heavy-handed censors. At this point, it might be useful to look at the United Nations Convention on the Rights of the

Child. It is extremely difficult to tell young people aged about sixteen or
so, who certainly have the capacity to become parents and may indeed
have become so, that they are in law, children. However, the designation is
clearly used in a protective manner, to indicate for example that young
people should not be made into child soldiers or executed.

The Convention was drafted before the advent of the internet but is
clear about mass media. A total of 192 countries in the UN out of 194 have
ratified the Convention, so it is important for us to know what it says,
particularly in those areas relevant to the use of ICT.

Article 13:   Children have the right to get and share information as
              long as that information is not damaging to them or to
              others.
Article 17:   Children have the right to reliable information from the
              mass media. Television, radio, and newspapers should
              provide information that children can understand, and
              must not promote materials that could harm children.
Article 28:   Children have a right to education. Discipline in schools
              must respect children's human dignity. Primary education
              should be free. Wealthy countries should help poorer
              countries achieve this.
Article 29:   Education must develop each child's personality and
              talents to the full. It should encourage children to respect
              their parents, and their own and other cultures.
Article 36:   Children must be protected from any activities that could
              harm their development.

References

Hoggart, R. (1996) *The Way We Live Now*. London: Random House.
International Center of Photography. www.icp.org/exhibitions/aftermath/
index.html
Marcus, S. (2000) Picture information literacy, in M. Monteith (ed.) *IT for Learning
Enhancement*. Exeter: Intellect.
OT: MadLibs spam (2003) http://weblogs.asp.net/cszurgot/archive/2003/12/18/
44453.aspx (accessed 18 December 2003).

9

LITERACY BEYOND THE CLASSROOM: YOUNG PEOPLE AND INTERNET USE

Kwok-Wing Lai

Introduction

Undoubtedly there has been a rapid growth of internet connectivity for home users in the last few years, and most of these users are teenagers. It is estimated that in 1999, 40 per cent of the 14 million American teenagers logged on to the internet on a typical day (Okrent 1999). No doubt the figure will be much higher today. In New Zealand, reportedly the most 'wired' country in the Pacific (Nielsen 1999), it was estimated that 43 per cent of its households would have a computer in 2000 (Ministry of Economic Development 2001). In a recent study (Lai, Pratt and Trewern 2001) evaluating the use of 25 secondary schools in the Otago region of New Zealand, it was reported that 76 per cent of the junior (aged 13–14) and 81 per cent of the senior (aged 15–17) students of these schools had a computer at home, and 60 per cent of the junior and 69 per cent of the senior students had internet connectivity.

With the advent of the World Wide Web to schools and homes, the concept of literacy has to be redefined to include skills of accessing, processing, and evaluating information gathered from the internet. However, some teachers and parents have not yet recognized quite how important it is for their children to acquire these skills. They are perhaps more concerned with speeding up internet connections in order for their children to gather more information, rather than reflecting on the question of why they need the information in the first place. Also, in the process of quick access to information, the quality of the information retrieved and whether it is appropriate or not to the learner or serves the original educational purposes are often overlooked. If literacy is about the skills young people need in order to function in the information society (Pachler 2001), it is essential for them to know how to evaluate the quality and appropriateness of the information retrieved from the internet. It is a challenge to all of us as teachers and parents which cannot be ignored.

While the internet has become an indispensable tool at home, offering many learning opportunities, its psychological and social effects on young users have not been adequately explored (Lai 2001a; Elliot 2001). For example, there has been an increasing concern that some of the information available on the internet may not be appropriate for young users. Internet pornography has drawn much media attention in recent years and has become so prolific that one report estimated that 800 million pornographic pages were archived on the web in 1999 (Hunter 2000). Neither can we ignore other websites, such as those related to occults, which have also become a concern lately. For example, the Association of Teachers and Lecturers in the UK has advised schools that the risks of delving into the occult on the internet should be communicated to students (*The Times* 2001). This does mean we are dealing with questions of value, but surely value judgments are necessarily included when we think of 'learning with the internet'. Whatever our individual thoughts about censorship in general, particularly when considering questions of literacy, we must at least encourage our children and students to develop a discriminating attitude towards what we consider inappropriate material on the internet. Possibly, when younger children are concerned, questions as to outright censorship may be raised.

The rapid growth of internet connectivity at home has led to debates as to how parents can best support their children in using the internet as an educational tool and yet also protect them from any harmful effects that might arise when they freely surf it. The following example concerning the law may sound over-dramatic and even scaremongering. However, there have been enough cases aired on the TV and in the press which indicate that internet access can bring trouble to young people. In allowing young users access to the internet, parents need to be concerned that they may be accessing materials which are not only harmful but also unlawful to have in one's possession. For example, in New Zealand, under present legislation (the Films, Videos, and Publications Classification Act 1993), it is unlawful to possess 'objectionable' materials (information, pictures, moving images and sound), which promote (a) the exploitation of children, or young persons, or both, for sexual purposes; or (b) the use of violence or coercion to compel any person to participate in, or submit to, sexual conduct; or (c) sexual conduct with or upon the body of a dead person; or (d) the use of urine or excrement in association with degrading or dehumanizing conduct or sexual conduct; or (e) bestiality; or (f) acts of torture or the infliction of extreme violence or extreme cruelty. Unfortunately, such sites are out there, not only waiting for a chancer-by but even reaching out to gain users, so we must review our responsibilities very carefully.

To reduce the chance of young users accessing these inappropriate or illegal websites, teachers and parents may have to impose some form of restriction or censorship on internet use. Parents need to come up with strategies to deal with objectionable material (legally defined) or inappropriate materials (from an ethical point of view) while being mindful of the importance of freedom of speech and privacy issues. They also need to understand the youth internet culture as well as the risks involved in using the internet as a means of communication (Facer, Sutherland, Furlong, and Furlong 2001). So, it's altogether a much more complex problem than perhaps we first envisaged.

While research has begun to report on how young people use the internet at home (for example, Facer et al. 2001), very little is known about how young people and their parents respond to objectionable or inappropriate materials out there on the web, their awareness of the risks involved in using the internet as a means of communication, as well as what strategies parents and guardians have successfully employed to deal with internet censorship. A study was conducted in New Zealand in 2000 to address some of these issues and some of the findings of this study are reported in this chapter.

How did students use the internet at home?

In this study two sets of questionnaires were sent to 66 New Zealand schools, distributed randomly to Year 7–12 (aged 11–16) students and their parents/caregivers who had home internet connections. A total of 1305 questionnaires were distributed. A total of 160 parents (male, 34.8 per cent; female, 65.2 per cent) and 176 students (44.3 per cent male, 55.7 per cent female) successfully completed the questionnaires. The participating students were categorized into junior students (aged 11–13, 58 per cent) and senior students (aged 14–16, 42 per cent). The response rates for students and parents were 25 per cent and 24 per cent, respectively. It should be noted that these response rates were lower than some other New Zealand studies conducted by the author in similar areas (Lai 2001a). The low response rates may reflect the lack of awareness of censorship issues related to internet use, and parents and young users thus were not prepared to respond to the questionnaires posted to them.

Using email

Overall close to 30 per cent of the students in this study used email at least daily at home, and another 30 per cent used it at least weekly. As expected, the senior students were more frequent users, with nearly half (43.4 per cent) of them using email at least daily or more at home, compared to only 20 per cent of the junior students. Only 1.3 per cent of the older students had never used email at home, compared to 12 per cent of the younger students. Students in this study most often emailed their school friends (73.8 per cent), family or relatives (61.3 per cent), and friends from other schools (41.4 per cent). It is clear from the survey that the use of email had greatly facilitated communication for this group of students. For example, one 11-year-old girl commented that she has sent email to: '[a] brother in England, sister in Sydney, sister in Dunedin, friends from school . . .'

When used at home, email was seldom used for school-related purposes, with nearly half of the students (42 per cent) reporting that they had never used email for school work. Notably just 8 per cent of the students frequently used it for school work. It is clear from the additional comments provided by 124 students that information communicated in emails was mainly socially oriented, aiming at 'catch[ing] up with friends'. The following is a typical example: 'I email to communicate with my friends and to organize social events such as 10-pin bowling' (male, aged 12).

Students used email to send 'cool stuff' and 'funny pictures' and 'funny stories and jokes' to each other. The following comment summarizes how students typically used email at home: 'I use email mainly to chat to friends and sometimes to get information for school work from friends' (female, aged 13).

Using the web

Over one-third (34.3 per cent) of the students reported that they used the web at least daily. On average, just over 53 per cent of the students used the web at least 30 minutes per day. There were quite a few heavy users in the group, however, with 6.4 per cent of the students using the web for at least 2 hours daily. Compared with use of email, more students used the web for school work, with 33 per cent of the junior and 47 per cent of the senior students frequently using the web for this purpose, presumably for project-related work. However, the web was most frequently used for leisure. Overall 58 per cent of the younger students and 68 per cent of the older students used it for leisure activities. Table 9.1 summarizes

Table 9.1 Percentages of students using the web at least daily or more

	Junior students	Senior students
Surfing	20.7	33.4
Net games	14.6	16.4
Download software	18.5	13.7
Download music	19.5	19.2

the percentages of students using the web at least daily or more for non-school-related activities.

Encountering inappropriate materials

With the huge media attention on pornographic websites, one would expect that students would come across these sites very frequently. However, it is evident from this study that it was not the case. Only a small percentage of students participating in this study had visited porno-graphic and other inappropriate websites, as can be seen from Table 9.2.

Table 9.2 Percentages of students having come across websites with inappropriate contents

	Overall	Junior students	Senior students
Violence	16.6	12.1	22.4
Explicit sex	18.3	12.1	26.3
Racism	5.7	2.0	10.5
Profanity	9.7	5.1	15.8
Horror	11.4	11.1	11.8
Crime	6.3	5.1	7.9
Cruelty	4.0	2.0	6.6
Cult	4.6	2.0	7.9
Drugs	7.4	4.0	11.8
Gambling	17.7	11.1	26.3
Bomb making	6.9	5.1	9.2

Senior students in this study in general had more frequent viewings of inappropriate materials on the web, as compared to younger students, as can be seen from Table 9.2. Nearly a quarter of the senior students had visited websites related to sex, gambling, and violence. Students also seemed to have little understanding of what illegal websites were, as defined in the New Zealand context, and three-quarters of the students had not visited one before.

In email communication, few students in this study had received emails containing inappropriate language or content. Except for chain mail, which nearly half (43 per cent) of the students have received at least once in the last six months, only between 7.3 and 13.8 per cent of the students had received email with racist, violent, abusive, threatening, gender-biased, or profane language. Only 7 per cent of the participants had received hate mail, and 5 per cent received mail with contents related to crime. When the data were further broken down by age, it is noted that senior students in general had received more inappropriate email than junior students, possibly because they used email more frequently (see Table 9.3).

Table 9.3 Percentages of students receiving inappropriate email in the last 6 months

	Junior students	Senior students
Hate mail	5.3	9.6
Chain mail	29.5	60.5
Racist language	9.5	5.4
Violent language	9.5	14.9
Abusive language	11.6	9.5
Threatening language	6.3	12.8
Gender biased language	6.3	12.8
Profane language	8.5	21.5
Related to crime	3.2	6.8
A virus	3.2	13.7

Understanding the risks of using the internet

It seems that many students in this study were unaware of the risks associated with internet use. Surely it is alarming to note that 35 per cent of the younger students and 32 per cent of the older students thought that there was no or little risk in using email. The percentages were even higher when it came to the use of the web, with 43 per cent of the younger students and 35 per cent of the older students considering there was no or little risk in using the web as a means of communication.

It is interesting to correlate the levels of awareness of the risks of internet use between those students and their parents. Even though the parents seemed to be more vigilant, nearly a quarter (23 per cent) of them regarded using email as risk free or with little risk, and close to 22 per cent held the same opinion when they used the web as a means of communication. It is possible that the parents' lack of awareness would have some impact on their children. However, statistically speaking, there was little correlation between the views of the students and parents (r = 0.064 for email, r = 0.139 for the web).

This lack of awareness of the risks involved in using the internet was also evident when the students were asked with whom they communicated. Over 30 per cent of the students had emailed someone they hadn't met before and nearly 40 per cent of the students had received email from someone they didn't know. According to one student: 'I email to people I have met on the WWW. These are friends from heat.net and certain web masters . . .' (male, aged 14).

Due to the lack of awareness, students divulged a great deal of personal information to strangers. Table 9.4 shows the percentages of students who provided strangers with personal information when they first communicated with them over the web.

Table 9.4 Percentages of students providing personal information to strangers

	Overall	Junior students	Senior students
Full name	19.6	22.4	17.2
Email address	35.5	32.7	37.9
Street address	2.8	2.0	3.4
Phone number	1.9	0.0	3.4
Age	80.4	71.4	87.9
Gender	81.3	69.4	91.4
School	15	10.2	19.0
Appearance	26.2	12.2	37.9
Interests	68.2	55.1	79.3

Overall younger students tended not to divulge as much information to strangers as older students. It is not clear what kind of language these students used when they communicated with strangers on the internet. However, it is interesting to note that over 93 per cent of the students had never heard of the term 'netiquette'.

One reason why students in this study had such a low level of awareness was perhaps because they had little experience in real-time chats, public bulletin board discussion, or newsgroup communication. Although 68 per cent of the older and 35 per cent of the younger students indicated they used chatrooms or ICQ as a means of communication, when further asked how often they used chatrooms, only a few more than 10 per cent of the younger students and 32 per cent of the older students used chatrooms weekly or more at home. As can be seen from Table 9.5, very few students had participated in bulletin board or newsgroup activities before.

Table 9.5 Percentages of students participating in public communication
at least weekly or more

	Overall	Junior students	Senior students
Chatroom	19.5	10.2	32.1
Bulletin boards	4.1	0	9.4
Newsgroup	8.3	5.3	11.8

Controlling access to the internet at home

Parents in this study were very aware of their responsibilities when allowing their children to access the internet at home. They understood that their parental role was to 'offer guidance to the child and monitor correct usage'.

As a parent it is my responsibility to censor my child's viewing of internet material that I consider to be inappropriate.
    To monitor my child's use of the internet, to discuss confusing or inappropriate messages or sites to help my child to make good choices for herself . . . To avoid inappropriate sites and excessive use.

So a child should not:

Access inappropriate sites (racist, sexual, violent etc). [My role is] to make sure she does not give personal information to anyone.

Or viewing:

Anything downgrading or oppressing another human being would offend me, use for education purposes is fine.

Parents also considered the use of the internet similar to use of other media.

Same as judging TV, movies etc. [It] is dependent on his age, under-standing of the issues after discussion with us (as parents), also his understanding that what is acceptable to a certain degree at home, is not acceptable elsewhere.

The purpose of monitoring was to protect their children. 'To keep children as safe as possible from the seedy side of the internet. Make sure they are aware of the chat lines . . .' or 'To protect my children from exposure to issues which they haven't the maturity to make satisfactory judgments on.'

Nearly three-quarters of the parents (72 per cent) reported that there were general rules about how their children should use computers at home. For example, the computers were to be used for certain purposes, and the most important one was for school work. As commented by one student:

> People doing homework have priority over those playing games, 30 minutes at most on the internet each day. People doing homework on the internet can be on the internet as long as they need it. (female, aged 14)

The internet also had to be used only at certain times. Students in general were allowed to use the computer only after they had completed their homework.

> I have to complete all my homework and piano before I can play on the computer (male, aged 12).

> Not allowed on it for more than 3 hours a day (male, aged 12).

Sometimes parents would use the internet as a reward. For example, 'I am only allowed on the computer when I get good marks' (male, aged 13).

The majority (74 per cent) of parents (and 64 per cent of the students as well) believed that censoring access to the internet, at least to some degree, was necessary. Over half (57 per cent) of the parents in this study reported that they had used some kind of strategies to limit their children's access to the internet at home. However, according to more than 62 per cent of the students, specific issues of internet censorship had seldom been discussed at home and 56 per cent of the students also reported that their families had not considered these issues to be important.

A number of strategies were employed to restrict access to inappropriate materials. The strategies parents used included:

Physical supervision

A total of 91 parents in this study provided additional information on the strategies they used to restrict access of their children to the internet. The most frequently cited strategy was supervision, which was mentioned by 53 parents (58 per cent).

> We are always keeping an eye on things. I am usually in the room . . .
> Walk to the computer frequently to check on the site she is in . . .

A couple of parents expressed that they didn't mind letting their children view these sites under their supervision, for 'educational purposes':

> It is better [for them] to learn and be aware of what is out there under my supervision rather than 'behind the bike shed' or doing it behind my back. My belief is that if educated extreme sites are of no fascination. If it is kept hidden then it becomes a big deal and they then spend a lot of time gorging at them to get thrills.

> [We had] open frank discussion . . . while surfing together questions pop up and hopefully answered . . . [we] access semi violent or sex sites together to stop them from being inquisitive . . .

Education

Of those parents who used a strategy to restrict their children's access to the internet, 42 per cent of them tried to educate and discuss with their children how they should behave when using the internet, sometimes in 'open communication in a relaxed way, not being up-tight and too restrictive in usage', but sometimes just 'tell[ing] them what can happen in the internet'. There was a widely held belief in this sample that educating youngsters with 'a good upbringing and installing such values that censorship is not necessary' was the way forward. One common strategy used by parents found in this study was for them to work together with their children in front of the computer. The following example illustrated the use of this strategy:

> We have open access to the internet, however I will look at what searches have been made or sites visited. On locating any of those sites visited I would discuss the site and why my child wanted to access it, openly discuss the issues, responsibilities and consequences.

Filtering software

Parents in this study were quite knowledgeable about the technical means of limiting their children's use of the internet. Half of them (37 per cent) knew about filtering software or how to check the history of the sites their children had visited (12 per cent). However, very few parents (8 per cent) actually used filtering software to restrict access, perhaps because they didn't consider it to be effective:

> [I] don't consider filtering software to be enough. Have heard where porno materials have been in educational sites and the Netnanny hasn't picked it up . . .

If the child wants to beat it they can. There was a case at my older sons school where they had a censor net on their internet and the child typed in a foreign word for 'sex' and accessed the sites . . .

Trust

While schools tend to impose hard and fast rules on limiting students' access to the internet (Lai 2001a), parents adopt different strategies, as can be seen from this study. Parents tended to communicate with the kids more effectively than teachers, taking the time to build up a sense of 'trust' in internet usage (Lai 2001a). As commented by parents:

There is an element of 'trust' – I believe it is important for him to know how to deal with this material whether I am there or not as sometimes it is totally unexpected.

son and I have good honest communication – he trusts me that I am not trying to stop him using the internet but showing them the consequences/pitfalls of internet use.

She knows I trust her. She is not upset when I occasionally browse over her shoulder. She understands why chatrooms are banned. She also has lots of other after school things . . . so doesn't have a lot of hours to waste surfing. Doesn't get bored and need to look for excitement of chatrooms etc.

Students also had similar responses:

My parents trust me more than the school trusts other kids. (female, aged 13)

The school has many rules that we have to follow otherwise we get banned but at home my parents just trust me. (female, aged 14)

How effective were the strategies?

Over half of the students (52.3 per cent) believed that to a large degree the overall strategies used by their parents in limiting their access to the internet were effective, and nearly three-quarters (73.4 per cent) of them had not encountered any problems with these strategies. The following is a typical response:

Knowing about the dangers has kept me from going further than appropriate . . . It's effective because I have seen what can happen with things such as internet stalking etc. This has put me off trying things that don't look safe. (female, aged 13)

As mentioned before, students in this study in general had little complaint about the restrictions imposed on their access to the internet at home. At least to some degree they believed that censorship was necessary (64 per cent) and over 90 per cent of the students felt that to some degree their parents had the right to determine what they were and were not allowed to access on the internet at home. 'It is a fair strategy, they have the right to supervise me' (female, aged 12).

Parents had similar responses: 66 per cent of the parents believed that to a large extent their strategies had been successful and 67 per cent of the parents had not experienced any problems with exercising those strategies. However, there is some doubt about the effectiveness of physical supervision as a strategy of limiting internet access as 71 per cent of the students reported that they were never or seldom supervised when they used the computer at home. The figure went even higher to 86 per cent for older students (61 per cent for the younger group).

Also, although parents thought that their strategies were effective, when asked whether their children had visited sites which were illegal or inappropriate for his or her age, nearly one-quarter of the parents gave the 'don't know' answer, indicating perhaps they had not monitored their children's internet access as closely as reported.

Students in this study were also asked how they compared the censorship strategies they had at home with those they had in school. Overall they preferred to access the internet from home because there was less control. About two-thirds of the students in this study reported that their schools had a tight control over how they used the internet. The control at home, however, was minimal, as can be seen from Table 9.6.

Table 9.6 Students comparing control of internet access between schools and homes, in percentages

	Low	Moderate	Extreme
School	12.6	20.8	66.7
Home	41.1	30.1	28.2

Other studies also have reported that internet censorship imposed in schools was very often resisted by students as imposing too much control over their use of the internet (Lai 2001a, 2001b; Lawson and Comber 2000).

Home and school link

Parents in this study were quite happy with the way their children were accessing the web and they considered their strategies in dealing with inappropriate materials to be quite successful. However, when they were asked whether they knew how their children used email in school, the majority replied that they had little knowledge of school use of email, as can be seen from Table 9.7.

Table 9.7 Percentages of parents who had knowledge of how their children used email

	No or little	Some	Large degree
What your child uses email for at home	11.2	21.8	66.9
Who your child emails from home	17.0	19.9	63.1
What your child uses email for at school	70.0	17.7	12.3
Who your child emails from school	77.2	10.6	12.1

Students were asked the same questions and their responses were similar to their parents. They confirmed that their parents had little knowledge of how they used the internet in school.

The fact that parents in this study lacked the knowledge of how their children used the internet in school made it difficult for them to come up with informed decisions as to how best they could support the teachers. Dealing with illegal or inappropriate websites is a complex issue, and parents have to work closely with teachers in order to come up with complementary strategies that can be used effectively both at home and in school.

It should be noted that the lack of knowledge of how their children used the internet in school was not due to the lack of computing knowledge. Parents in this study were asked to self-evaluate their levels of computer and internet literacy. The Table 9.8 shows parents' levels of computer and internet literacy, in percentages.

Table 9.8 Computer and internet literacy of parents, in percentages

	Low	Moderate	High
Computer literacy	15.3	38.9	45.8
Internet literacy	17.8	36.9	44.3

As can be seen from Table 9.8, nearly half of the parents considered themselves to be highly computer and internet literate, which suggests that there was no lack of knowledge or interest in computing. In fact, in this study 92 per cent of the parents used email, and 65 per cent of them used it at least once a day or more often. They were also active web users, with 93 per cent of them using the web and nearly 40 per cent of them using it at least once a day or more frequently. Also, 39 per cent of them used the web at least 30 minutes or more a day. They mostly used it as an educational tool (87 per cent), followed by leisure activities (79 per cent). However, similar to students, very few parents used the internet for many-to-many communication. The majority of the parents also have never used chatrooms (81 per cent), bulletin boards (80 per cent) or participated in newsgroups (72 per cent).

Conclusion

In this information era, we need to move beyond the traditional notion of literacy, towards a critical media literacy (Pachler 2001), which includes skills and tools young people have to acquire to evaluate text, sound, and images that are readily accessible from the internet. In this chapter we have documented the strategies employed by a group of New Zealand parents in response to the availability of inappropriate material on the web, which may be harmful for their children to view or use. As teenagers increasingly have the need to access the internet for information gathering and for leisure, it is important to come up with effective strategies to support or limit their internet access as well as to understand how they would respond to these strategies.

In this study we have noted that parents preferred physical supervision and education as the means of protecting their children from viewing and using illegal or inappropriate materials on the web. Students found these strategies fair and not limiting and they had few problems with them. Although parents considered these strategies successful, the fact that they knew very little about how their children used the web as a source of information and as a medium of communication suggests that their children were not as closely monitored as was thought.

However, it should be noted that strategies taken by parents could be very different from those in schools. As pointed out by McKenzie (1995):

The choice for schools is different . . . than for parents, in that schools must come up with procedures which meet the needs of the full spectrum of students, while parents may customize their family internet access to meet family values.

Thus, although this chapter has described and summarized the censorship strategies used by a group of parents, it should be noted that strategies used by individual parents are largely dependent on their values and philosophies as to how their children should be brought up. For some, no specific strategies are needed, as was pointed out by a parent:

I don't happen to think that a strategy is required as the internet is only a small part of teaching a child the 'rights and wrongs' of growing up. It is part of the overall strategy.

Acknowledgement

This study was funded by an Otago Research Grant (LAM B14). The author wishes to acknowledge the assistance of Dr Keryn Pratt and Phil Munro in the data collection process.

References

Elliot, A. (2001) The wired school: legal, ethical and social issues, in K.W. Lai (ed.) *e-Learning: Teaching and Professional Development with the Internet*, pp. 155–82. Dunedin: The University of Otago Press.

Facer, K., Sutherland, R., Furlong, R. and Furlong, J. (2001) What's the point of using computers? The development of young people's computer expertise in the home, *New Media and Society*, 3(2): 199–219.

Hunter, C.D. (2000) Internet filter effectiveness – Testing over- and underinclusive blocking decisions of four popular web filters, *Social Science Computer Review*, 18(2): 214–22.

Lai, K.W. (2001a) Internet in the classroom: teachers as custodians? in H. Taylor and P. Hogenbirk (eds) *Information and Communication Technologies in Education: The School of the Future*. Boston: Kluwer.

Lai, K.W. (2001b) Role of the teacher, in H. Adelsberger, B. Collis and J. Pawlowski (eds) *Handbook on Information Technologies for Education and Training*. Berlin: Springer-Verlag.

Lai, K.W. (in press) Health risks with teachers' computer use: some New Zealand observations, *Journal of Information Technology in Teacher Education*.

Lai, K.W., Pratt, K. and Trewern, A. (2001) *Learning with Technology: Evaluation of the Otago Technology Project*. Dunedin: The Community of Otago Trust.

Lawson, T. and Comber, C. (2000) Censorship, the Internet and schools: A new moral panic? *The Curriculum Journal*, 11(2): 273–85.

McGrory, D. (2001) Children seduced by forces of Satanism on the Internet, *The Times*, 28 August.

McKenzie, J. (1995) Protecting our children from the Internet, *From Now On*, 4(10). www.fro.org/fnojun95.html

Ministry of Economic Development (2001) *Computers in Homes*. Available at: www.med.govt.NewZealand/pbt/infotech/itstats2001/itstats2001-05.html# P328_24663

Nielsen, A.C. (1999) *New Zealand Leads Asia Pacific's Cyberspace Advance*. www.eratings.com/news/19991118htm

Okrent, D. (1999) Raising kids online: What can parents do? *Time*, 10 May: 42–7.

Pachler, N. (2001) Connecting schools and pupils: To what end? in M. Leask (ed.) *Issues in Teaching Using ICT*. London: Routledge.

INDEX

Related books from Open University Press
Purchase from www.openup.co.uk or order through your local bookseller

NEW LITERACIES
CHANGING KNOWLEDGE AND CLASSROOM LEARNING
Colin Lankshear and Michele Knobel

An intriguing book which argues why the use of new media is transforming ways of knowing and making meaning in the digital age. Essential reading for anyone who cares about literacy education.

Associate Professor Ilana Snyder, Monash University

A good book opens a window onto new vistas; an excellent one, on the other hand, pulls readers through the opening and beyond, inviting critical dialogue at every turn. *New Literacies* belongs in the excellent catagory.

Donna Alvermann, University of Georgia

Literacy education continues to be dominated by a mindset that has passed its use-by date. Education has failed to take account of how much the world has changed during the information technology revolution. It proceeds as though the world is the same as before – just somewhat more technologised. This is the hallmark of an 'outsider' mindset. In fact, qualitatively new literacies and new kinds of knowledge associated with digitally saturated social practices abound. 'Insiders' understand this, 'outsiders' do not. Yet 'outsider' perspectives still dominate educational directions. Meanwhile, student 'insiders' endure learning experiences that mystify, bemuse, alienate and miseducate them.

This book describes new social practices and new literacies, along with kinds of knowledge associated with them. It shows what is at stake between 'outsider' and 'insider' mindsets, argues that education requires a shift in mindset, and suggests how and where pursuit of progressive change might begin.

Contents
Foreword – Part one: What's new? – From 'reading' to the 'new literacy studies' – The 'new literacy studies' and the study of new literacies – Atoms and bits: Literacy and the challenge of mindsets – Part two: Staring at the future – Faking it: The national grid for learning – Attention economics, information and new literacies – The ratings game: From eBay to Plastic – Part three: Changing knowledge – Digital epistemologies: Rethinking knowledge for classroom learning – New ways of knowing: Learning at the margins – Bibliography – Index.

240pp   0 335 21066 X (Paperback)   0 335 21067 8 (Hardback)

TEACHING MULTILITERACIES ACROSS THE CURRICULUM
CHANGING CONTEXTS OF TEXT AND IMAGE IN CLASSROOM PRACTICE

Len Unsworth

Teaching literacy in today's primary and junior secondary schools involves both teaching children what people understand as traditional literacy and also teaching children how to read and produce the kinds of texts typical of the current and emerging information age. This still means understanding grammar as a functional tool in reading and writing but it also now necessarily entails explicit knowledge about how images and layout can be structured in different ways to make different kinds of meanings and how both text and image are used in electronic formats. This major new textbook outlines the basic theoretical knowledge teachers need to have about visual and verbal grammar and the nature of computer-based texts in school learning. In doing so it:

- addresses both the present demands in literacy teaching and the emerging demands for teaching the multiliteracies of the information age;
- provides accessible, integrative, classroom oriented coverage of the complex range of current and emerging issues (like teaching grammar, visual literacy, the role of computer-based information and communication technology, critical literacy, literacies and learning in English and other curriculum areas);
- includes both theoretical frameworks and detailed practical guidelines with examples of classroom work;
- deals with the continuities and differences in the teaching of infants, children in the primary school and the transition to the first years of secondary education.

Contents

Introduction – Changing dimensions of school literacies – Learning about language as a resource for literacy development – Describing visual literacies – Distinguishing the literacies of school science and humanities – Exploring multimodal meaning-making in literature for children – Developing multiliteracies in the early school years – Developing multiliteracies in content area teaching – Teaching multiliteracies in the English classroom – References – Index.

320pp   0 335 20604 2 (Paperback)   0 335 20605 0 (Hardback)

CLASSROOM INTERACTIONS IN LITERACY

Eve Bearne, Henrietta Dombey and Teresa Grainger

- How important is professional knowledge and an informed understanding of pedagogy?
- What are the key issues in the unfolding language and literacy agenda?
- How can the profession encompass a more interactive and informed view of pedagogy?

This book examines some of the complexities and debates about language, literacy and learning, challenging current assumptions about shared understanding of pedagogical principles. It foregrounds social and cultural issues and the nature of interaction between children and teachers; children and children; children and texts of all kinds; and the significance of wider interactions within the teaching profession.

The contributors revitalise debate about the nature of professional knowledge, provide insights into the detail of classroom discourse and teacher interventions, and examine the transformative possibilities of literacy. They argue for a more open and expansive agenda informed by an analytically constructive view of pedagogy and challenge the profession to move from restrictive certainties to the potent possibilities of development through uncertainty and risk.

Classroom Interactions in Literacy is key reading for primary teachers, students in initial teacher education, teacher educators, researchers in the field, literacy consultants in LEAs, inspectors and advisors.

Contents

Contributors

Robin Alexander, Evelyn Arizpe, Eve Bearne, Kathy Coulthard, Henrietta Dombey, Peter Geekie, Teresa Grainger, Charmian Kenner, Trinka Messenheimer, Angela Packwood, Louise Poulson, Sandra Smidt, Ilana Snyder, Morag Styles, Sam Twiselton, Gordon Wells.

232pp   0 335 21385 5 (Paperback)   0 335 21386 3 (Hardback)